COMPLETE

ATHLETE

...

BASEBALL

2018

COMPLETE ATHLETE, LLC
660 Newport Center Dr., Suite 200
Newport Beach, CA 92660
Phone: (714) 949-3845
www.mycompleteathlete.com

*To every young athlete playing baseball and aspiring to be a **COMPLETE ATHLETE** in every aspect of your life—this book is for you.*

TABLE OF CONTENTS

INTRODUCTION

DO YOU DREAM OF BECOMING THE NEXT BUSTER POSEY? DEREK JETER? CLAYTON KERSHAW?

If you are determined to learn how high-character athletes got to be that way, earn a college scholarship, or possibly become a professional baseball player, this book can help show you the way to become a **COMPLETE ATHLETE**.

Being a **COMPLETE ATHLETE** is about so much more than just having the best stats on your team or about playing for a paycheck, though; it is about developing character and competing with integrity. If you make growing your leadership skills as much a priority as you do your technical skills, you will become a more responsible individual, a better teammate, and a more balanced person while you also become a stronger athlete. By working on your attitude and mind as well as your body, you will come to understand what the **COMPLETE ATHLETE** really means—and why it matters so much.

This book will help you prepare to play baseball at the highest levels AND be a desirable recruit for college and/ or professional coaches. It emphasizes the concept that success is not just dependent on one's natural ability; it is also influenced by attitude and behavior, as well as how you treat yourself and others, both on and off the field of play. Guidelines, suggestions, and real-life examples are provided by our team of experts, whom you can read about at the end of this book.

A youth athlete who is determined to earn a college scholarship and/or become a professional baseball player must become a **COMPLETE ATHLETE**.

There are five levels to becoming a **COMPLETE ATHLETE**. Generally speaking, the five levels correspond to the following (although there may be some overlap):

Level 1 - Elementary school athlete
Level 2 - Middle school athlete
Level 3 - High school athlete
Level 4 - College athlete
Level 5 - Professional athlete

A **COMPLETE ATHLETE** must also achieve the highest level in five different categories:

ATTITUDE refers to how you behave on the field. For instance, listening quietly while your coach is talking and showing respect for your fellow players demonstrate that you have a good attitude.

PREPARATION refers to off-the-field activities, including eating right and getting enough sleep, keeping your uniform clean and equipment well maintained, practicing, and more.

FITNESS refers to the physical fitness needed to compete in your sport.

TECHNIQUE revolves around skill level, including mastering the basics and specializing in a particular position.

LIFESTYLE refers to how you treat yourself, including eating right and getting enough sleep. It also includes getting good grades and being a good member of your family and your community.

THE COMPLETE ATHLETE MATRIX

ATTITUDE
- Respect
- Sportsmanship
- Teamwork
- Professionalism
- Leadership

PREPARATION
- Practice
- Nutrition
- Hydration
- Recovery
- Mentality

FITNESS
- Lower-Body Strength
- Upper-Body Strength
- Flexibility/Mobility
- Core Strength
- Speed/Quickness/ Endurance

TECHNIQUE
- Throwing
- Hitting
- Infield Fielding
- Outfield Fielding
- Game Assessment

LIFESTYLE
- Family
- Academics
- Social Life
- Role Model
- Living Your Sport

Each pillar holds up a category that contributes to the overall development and character of a **COMPLETE ATHLETE**. "Character," according to *Merriam-Webster*, is "the way someone thinks, feels, and behaves." All of these aspects influence what kind of person and player you are.

If you look at the chart above, you'll see that several categories have attributes that relate to your actions off the field. That's because what you do off the field affects how you play on the field. For example, maintaining good fitness will make a big difference in your ability to perform the techniques needed to play baseball.

The key? Just because someone is a professional player in the sense of being paid to play, he might not be considered a professional according to this system.

The next few sections of this book will discuss what you need to know, do, and be at each succeeding level to become a **COMPLETE ATHLETE**.

DEAR PARENTS,

I know you want to be as supportive as possible. You want to provide your son with every opportunity to succeed and every tool to help get him there. You want to help take his talent as far as possible. This book is here to help you do that, and here is your first insider's secret: don't focus solely on his improvement on the field.

It is undeniably, unquestionably, universally true that young men who are well-rounded in their academic and personal life will be mentally healthier in their athletic life, and baseball is very much a mental game. When your children are young, don't miss vacations, family events, and non-baseball-related fun time because you feel pressure to help add another tournament win and your son happens to be the best player.

As a personal coach, the No. 1 question I am asked is, "What can we do to increase my son's chances of getting a scholarship?" My No. 1 answer is, "Focus on getting him academically qualified." All the baseball talent in the world won't matter if your son gets benched for being academically ineligible. College coaches don't want to be babysitters, staying on top of players to keep their grades up. To get better on the field, you have to focus on getting better off the field. That's not to say that every athlete will be able to make straight A's or should avoid receiving professional coaching outside normal requirements from team practice but every student-athlete needs to have the maturity to realize that he is a student before he is an athlete—and he needs to have parents who reinforce this.

As a baseball parent, one of the most difficult things you have to do is to filter out the noise from all the different sources, or you will find yourself constantly second-guessing decisions and sinking time and money into a seemingly bottomless pit of showcases, special events, and more and more private training. Please don't compare and measure your son's success to others of the same age because this is a time of growing physically and mentally, and everyone is on different tracks than your son. It will never be a fair measuring gauge and will only cause sleepless nights. Whenever one young man gets a scholarship offer, signs with a school, or is drafted, all the other parents tend to panic and question what they are doing wrong. What do they need to do to get their son noticed? Do they need to pull him from his current team or school and put him with a different coach? He's just as good an athlete as the other boy. He's even better at his position. He had higher stats … What they don't see is the whole picture. Maybe the other boy knew a coach, had an alumni connection or better grades, or has hit a growth spurt. Perhaps the coach recognized some other unquantifiable quality about him other than numbers.

Stop. Please, for the sake of your son, for the sake of your own sanity, for the sake of the game itself. You are not doing anyone a favor when you panic in front of your son or throw more money at the situation. I know that the competition can seem daunting, but when you feel overwhelmed, take a step back and look at the big picture. Did your son's national ranking just drop because someone logged an 83 mph fastball and your son took a break to rest his arm after logging an 82 weeks earlier? Don't automatically think you need to sign up for the next showcase or speed up his throwing program ASAP. Instead, realize that coaches understand how baseball works and how statistics are registered. Instead of panicking, remind yourself that your son is being viewed in the same pool of players who post similar—not just identical—numbers. Pushing him into another special event when his arm isn't rested or he is falling behind on his schoolwork can do more harm than good and ultimately slow the process.

Always remember that you are your son's best advocate. You are the one who is in the best position to protect him, encourage him, and challenge him. It can be difficult for a child battling an overuse injury to refuse when a coach insists he needs to play another game. That's when you need to step in and say no. It can be challenging when a child feels discouraged because he had a bad game or he is smaller than everyone else and thinks he should give up even though he loves the game. That's when you need to step in and encourage him to keep chasing his dream. It can be upsetting when your child needs to be benched as motivation to get his grades up, but if you really care about his whole development—as a person instead of just as a baseball player—that may be the call you need to make, even if it upsets him or angers his coach. You are the parent and you know best.

You are a key aspect in raising your child to be more than just a series of numbers on a recruiter's clipboard. You are an essential part in his journey to becoming a **COMPLETE ATHLETE**, and I applaud you for making this commitment.

Sincerely,
Dave Coggin

DEAR ATHLETE,

You are chasing scholarships and career goals, and your dedication is admirable. But no matter what level you have reached, whether just starting out on your first team or entering the pros, don't forget to be a kid.

For better or worse, in recent years, baseball has become a sport where one specializes early, plays year-round, and obsesses about statistics or rankings at even the youngest levels. This has resulted in much higher numbers of injuries, not necessarily better athletes. Players come back from injuries too soon because they fear they will fall behind and, as a result, reinjure themselves. If they are not performing at an elite level in middle school, they worry that their chances of ever playing in college or going pro are already over. They believe that they have to find one position and stick to it, or they will never become skilled enough to move up. And in the midst of all of this stress and worry, they lose something absolutely essential: They forget how to enjoy the game.

You are not a robot, nor were you intended to function like one. Of course, you need to have tremendous discipline to train and focus when you take the field. But you will never be a truly great player if you don't know how to play loose, listen to your instincts, and break out of a rigid view of your one specific role.

As you get older, the pressure only increases as everyone races to get recruited first. Young men who develop faster physically tend to get more playing time and spark more interest. Those who take longer to develop often get frustrated or bored because they are not playing as much. Sometimes, they even get shuffled out of the system by coaches who only want to focus on their "stars." Here is a word of advice: your coach deserves your respect and best effort, but your coach is not the end word on your career path.

Don't let anyone insist you have to specialize early. That may actually make it harder, not easier, for you to succeed. Don't let anyone tell you that your future is at risk if you play more than one sport or position. Players who diversify become mentally tougher, learn to respect different coaching styles, are less likely to face injury, are less likely to burn out, develop different skill sets and muscle responses, and are of more value to college coaches and professional scouts.

You picked up this book because you care about baseball and your future in it. In the following pages, we will discuss technical tips, lifestyle choices, winning habits from top performers on and off the field, when to rest, how to get your arm in shape, steps to recruitment, and all the different components that go into becoming a **COMPLETE ATHLETE**. Every aspect of your game is important, from your batting stance to your pitching technique or fielding skills to your speed and agility. But your game is more than the numbers you post; your game is also the joy it brings to you as you smell the grass, hear the cheers, and listen for the crack of the bat. Don't ever forget to be a kid.

Sincerely,
Dave Coggin

DEAR COACHES,

You have an incredibly difficult job. I realize that you are already very much aware of this, but I think it is worth acknowledging. Some of you are paid professionals who lead elite teams, some of you are high school coaches who manage teams on top of teaching careers, and some of you are volunteers who want to help your son's baseball dreams or just give something back to your community. No matter what, you have two major factors driving your decisions: You want to do what is best for your team, and you want to do what is best for your individual players. Unfortunately, the two do not always align.

I understand the tension.

On the one hand, you have to think about the team. When you play your best athletes, you generally win more. When you win more, your sponsorships improve, resulting in better equipment, more showcases, and more talented recruits. The whole team benefits.

On the other hand, you are supposed to be looking out for your players' best interests. If a kid can never pitch in your high school games because he wears out his arm every weekend throwing for his travel ball league, what is he contributing to the team? You know he needs to rest and recover, but you also know you have your district championship coming up and need to count on your talent. What is the right call?

Then there is the issue of kids transferring to other teams or schools to play for other coaches. How would you react if one of your star players decided he was a better fit on a different team? Would you bad-mouth him to recruiters for letting you down, or would you respect his or his parents' decision to make his own choices about what is best for him?

You have to ask yourself which concerns you most: the health and future of your athletes or your own bottom line? I know that sounds harsh, but as coaches, it is something we should be constantly weighing. What is the real motivation behind your decisions? What drives you to make the coaching calls that do? If you aren't demonstrating character and integrity, why should you expect your players to do so?

Ultimately, if you are a leader who genuinely cares about what is best for each player and are willing to put your own win-loss record on the line to do right by them, you will have loyal athletes and parents. Sometimes, that means accommodating a player's request for time off for an injury; other times, that means benching him as a form of discipline. Sometimes, you must tell him to hustle when he is being lazy; other times, you gently counsel him when he is going through personal challenges. It may even mean kicking his tail when he needs a little perspective.

It can be a tricky line to walk, but it comes down to trust, which is essential between coaches and athletes. Educate yourself on overuse injuries and recommended periods of play versus rest. Know the signs of fatigue, and communicate with parents to have a sense of what the last six months have looked like, not just the last six days. When a child feels protected and valued, he will do better overall. If players and parents trust that you truly have their best interests at heart, they will show you loyalty. Even if the worst case scenario for your team does happen and an athlete decides to play for another team, you need to remember that talent is everywhere. It is your job, as a coach, to find it, foster it, and help each child develop his potential to become a **COMPLETE ATHLETE**.

Sincerely,
Dave Coggin

IN LEVEL 1

A baseball player is most impressionable and has a great, innocent love for the game. Parents have a huge influence on their children's habits, and coaches in Level 1 are an extension of great parenting in teaching the finer points of baseball. This chapter will help bring athletes, parents, and coaches together to start building a consistent and strong foundation. Here you will be guided to build this foundation, learning basic tools to have the most safe, enjoyable experience as you begin a long baseball journey.

1.1 ATTITUDE

A **POSITIVE ATTITUDE** is essential to an athlete's success both on and off the playing field, especially as he moves into higher levels of play. In fact, college coaches seek out athletes who display positive attitudes.

A positive attitude is something that can be developed with practice, just like any other skill. A **COMPLETE ATHLETE** makes a habit of demonstrating the following five attributes:

RESPECT

SPORTSMANSHIP

TEAMWORK

PROFESSIONALISM

LEADERSHIP

RESPECT

Showing **RESPECT** means treating others in ways that show they have worth and value and being considerate of other people's feelings. At Level 1, youth baseball players should always treat their coaches with respect. These are the people who have taken time out of their busy lives to pass on their love for and knowledge of baseball and provide opportunities for players to learn more about the game and play well. For these same reasons, players should treat all game officials with respect as well.

HOW TO DEMONSTRATE RESPECT
FOR YOUR COACHES »

- When you arrive at a game or practice, greet your coach politely.
- Find out how your coach prefers to be addressed, whether by his or her first name, by Mr. or Mrs. _____, or simply as Coach. Always address your coach the way he or she prefers.
- Listen carefully and don't fidget when your coaches are speaking.
- When your coaches are speaking directly to you, look them in the eye and don't interrupt.
- Don't talk back or sass your coaches or game officials.
- Follow directions without complaining; in other words, do what you're told to do.

ATHLETES » You can stand out in a lot of different ways, and I don't mean just on the field. I can recall one player in particular that stood out by just how he entered a room. He was one of the most talented kids in our younger training groups, which comprised mostly seventh- and eighth-graders, but he was only in the sixth grade. He carried himself with confidence and an ability to light up the room. He was wise beyond his years already.

His energy was contagious. You would see athletes who were normally quiet and reserved go right over to him, high-five him, and start laughing and smiling. When I would watch him from across the gym, I would see him absolutely kill an exercise with all his energy and then recover and encourage his workout partner to do more weight or try to get one more rep. You couldn't catch him without a big smile during the time he was around you.

I asked his travel ball coach, "Is he always like this?" The coach said, "Without a doubt. There is something special about him. Even when he isn't having a great game at the plate, he just finds a way to help us win with a great defensive play or just hustling after anything and everything."

Even though he was so young, he did something every athlete should do when he entered the gym: he approached the coaches with a strong handshake and even asked how their day was. Not hard to tell this kid had a great support system at home, and his parents had done an amazing job. This type of maturity and positive energy helped make him a **COMPLETE ATHLETE**.

There are some important lessons here. At some point, coaches are going to evaluate kids to see if they are well-rounded athletes. Coaches think about more than a player's on-field performance. They will start to see what kind of person they are bringing into their program and if he will represent them well. By learning to approach coaches and act respectfully toward them now, players will make a good, lasting impression.

JOIN THE CONVERSATION!

For more stories and conversations with athletes and coaches, download the **COMPLETE ATHLETE** app!

SPORTSMANSHIP

Good **SPORTSMANSHIP** starts with respect for one's teammates, opponents, coaches, and officials.

It also includes playing with integrity: following the rules and never cheating.

At Level 1, a youth baseball player should be familiar enough with the basic rules of the game to always play by those rules. (To review basic rules, go to Appendix 1.) He should never try to bend the rules or cheat. In addition, he should always abide by what the coaches and officials say in terms of penalties and refrain from arguing with them. After all, they know more than he does when it comes to what's fair and what's not in the game of baseball.

PARENTS » Sportsmanship applies to parents, too. At this level, parents have so much influence over the direction their son will go, how baseball feels to him, and how he will remember the sport as he looks back on his younger playing days.

One thing we see too much, unfortunately, is parents who disregard how they look, sound, and approach every situation they believe to be negative, problems they think should be fixed, or perceived slights against their child.

Quite often, kids who have issues such as burning out or not wanting to play anymore are the ones whose parents stand right next to the batter's box yelling at umpires or put their head in the dugout to question a coach about why they made this move or why they pulled someone out or why he is batting in the sixth spot instead of the third spot.

The parents think their kid is as tough as they are and can handle all that. Most of the time, however, what we see is a kid who resents his parents as he grows up. As he gets further along in baseball, he doesn't want to share things with them or his family. Frequently, he decides he doesn't want to play anymore because he's just so tired of having to deal with his parents.

Many times, parents don't see that; they believe they are doing what's best for their child. But if they were to take a step back and see themselves and how they act, they might react differently to situations. They don't need to get upset about every bad pitch, every missed ground ball, or each 0-4 at the plate. They don't scrutinize every position on the field where they think their son should be starting. Every time they do this, they are teaching their child to become as cynical and negative as they sound. Let kids fail and learn. Teach them in these moments that it's not how many times they fall but how many times they get back up. Parents need to know there may be valid reasons beyond their understanding as to why their kid is not playing a certain position.

There are also some amazing parents on the opposite end of the spectrum who have such a refreshing approach with how they handle the exact same situations: bad calls, their kid not playing his favorite position, etc. They really listen to what the coach is saying and give the player space to handle it his own way. This is such a valuable thing to learn in baseball, where there are going to be situations that aren't ideal. Players have to learn how to either handle them or move past them. These parents tend to sit farther back in the stands, stay out of the dugout, stay away from the fence, and make only positive comments to coaches and their child's teammates. (This can be great!)

Some parents even stay out of their child's line of vision the entire game so he can do his thing; they wait until it's appropriate to talk about the game and even avoid bringing it up until their son initiates it. One of the best things you can ask an athlete after a tough loss or outing is, "Do you want to grab some food?"

COACH MIKE MARTIN » *Some youth leagues are no longer allowing parents at games. Coaches have reached their limits of disrespect and fussing from parents and have basically told them, "Sorry, but we've got them now. We will teach them to play the game. We don't want you here." Now, parents aren't allowed at practices and most games. And you know what? I don't blame them. Unfortunately, there are a lot of parents these days who need classes in how to treat their children when it comes to athletics. When my son was growing up, I never told him, "You've got to do this; you've got to do that." I only told him to play the game right. I did not fuss at him. None of the parents did. But now, many parents fuss at their children, fuss at the coaches, fuss at the umpires. That's something that needs to be addressed because it's not good for anyone, and it is setting a terrible example for the children.*

TEAMWORK

TEAMWORK means working together as a group in order to achieve a goal. In sports, players contribute their individual skills and efforts in cooperation with their teammates to win games.

At Level 1, youth baseball players learn what it means to play as part of a team, not just as an individual athlete, a skill that is important at every level of play.

To pass Level 1, a youth baseball player must always share responsibilities with other players and never make it all about him during games. He also must cooperate when coaches allow everyone, of all skill levels, to participate.

PROFESSIONALISM

Certainly, a youth baseball player is not a professional in the sense of being paid to play. However, developing the attitude and behaviors of a professional can help him more easily move up through the levels.

Many professional fields require some kind of proper attire and appearance. For example, most lawyers wear suits. Many doctors wear white coats. At Level 1, a youth baseball player should always arrive on time with all his equipment at hand. He should also have a neat and clean appearance, including a uniform that has been recently washed and shoes that are properly tied.

It is important that parents remember to act professionally as well. They need to treat other players, coaches, and their own children with respect and control their emotions at games and practices.

TIP » Never allow anyone but yourself to carry your baseball equipment or bags to and from practices, games, or tournaments. Please do it yourself.

COACHES » I have always been impressed with the type of coach who puts extra effort into a Little League team's practices and games. This type of coach plans ahead of practice, studies or reads books on how to make practice more efficient, and pushes players to skill levels they didn't think they could reach. This type of coach adds higher-level drills and plays in practice and works with players throughout the week so they can use them in games. During the four years I played in Upland Foothill Little League, there was a team that always had a reputation for being the top in the league. Everything they did was different. It was so organized, from the way they all came down to the field together, to how they always had their uniforms on properly and wore their team jackets. They looked like a team that had already thought about how they were going to approach every little detail for each game. When it came to game time, there was an air about them—you felt as though they were going to beat you before they even got on the field.

Those coaches ended up leading the All-Star team, and when I played for them, I got to see right off the bat why they were so good. We worked on many more skills than I ever had with any other team. The coaches came up with plays and had different signals for each one. They asked us to understand and do things above our age level. However, they made it work by being patient with us and making sure we understood concepts, often watching examples from games on TV the previous night. They did not just put together practices; they studied professional games and implemented what they saw in our practice. It was evident how seriously those high-level coaches took their job, even working with 11- and 12-year-olds. It's not that we were the most talented team, but it was how we practiced, how we moved, and how we handled situations, whether putting a bunt down or moving runners. We practiced all the little things, the fundamentals, as part of our daily routine. As All-Stars, we came to understand the importance of doing the little things over and over.

We acted the way our coaches taught us to, as if Joe Torre had come down to coach us. These coaches worked hard to make sure we played above our level—and gave us the confidence to do so.

LEADERSHIP

A good leader is able to inspire and motivate others to do things they would not normally do, or to perform better than they would on their own. Developing leadership skills can benefit a youth athlete not only in high school and college but in their professional lives as well.

At Level 1, a youth baseball player is not expected to take on a leadership role. However, by watching how his coaches inspire and motivate the team, he can begin to develop an understanding of leadership traits, both effective and ineffective.

COACHES >> Kids at this age are too young to take on big leadership roles; however, some can begin to slowly develop these skills. The coach plays a huge role in influencing this.

Frankly, coaches provide the best examples of leadership at this level. During the Little League World Series a few years back, there was a moment that exemplified what a good coach does to show leadership. LLWS games are televised, which puts the kids under tremendous pressure; the TV cameras zoom on the kids as though they're 25-year-old professionals.

One moment that stays in my mind involved a pitcher giving up a lot of runs. He simply wasn't having a good game, and you could tell he was falling apart when his coach came out to the mound. Now, the coach could have been like a lot of Little League coaches who scream or who don't say anything and just take the ball while the kid walks back to the dugout with his head down—that type of leadership can be even worse than yelling at the kids.

Too many coaches at this level use body language to tell players they aren't getting the job done. It plays a huge role that coaches have to be aware of, especially at this level. This coach, however, had great body language as he came out to the mound. The coach remained positive, even though it was in the middle of one of the worst games of the team's season.

He knelt down next to the pitcher and told him how proud he was of him, how far he had come, how well he had done. The coach wasn't concerned about the game spiraling out of control; instead, he was trying to lift up the pitcher.

That moment was shared all over the place, including being shown on ESPN over and over again. It went viral on social media. At that moment, the coach showed leadership, and the world got to see and learn from it. It was a pivotal moment in that kid's life and a prime example of how coaches can shape their players' lives off the baseball field as well as on it.

1.2 PREPARATION

PREPARATION refers to off-the-field activities, such as practicing skills, eating right, staying hydrated, getting enough rest, and mentally preparing for a game or practice. Coaches love athletes who prepare: these are the players who are eager to learn, eager to play, and ultimately, eager to win. They are the athletes that coaches want to help succeed because they already have a winning attitude. Preparation also helps athletes feel positive and confident in their ability to perform.

A **COMPLETE ATHLETE** prepares to perform on the field of play by continuously improving on the following:

PRACTICE

NUTRITION

HYDRATION

RECOVERY

MENTALITY

PRACTICE

At Level 1, baseball should revolve around having fun, getting exercise, and learning to be part of a team. Nonetheless, **PRACTICE** is essential for becoming skilled at the techniques of the sport. Practicing also helps a youth athlete avoid injuries and become a better, more confident player.

Team practices usually occur several times per week. They are run by the coaches, who plan activities based on the techniques they believe the team needs to work on. Individual practice is performed by a youth athlete outside of regularly scheduled team sessions without the coach and team present.

HOW MUCH TIME TO PRACTICE »

There is little agreement on the exact amount of time a youth athlete should practice on his own. Most experts agree that it's better to be fully engaged in practice for a shorter period rather than mindlessly performing many different techniques over long sessions. In other words, the type of practice is more important than the amount of time spent practicing. When a youth athlete is able to do the same skill over and over again consistently, he has mastered that skill. As Bruce Lee once said, "I don't fear the man who has practiced 10,000 kicks once, but I fear the man who has practiced one kick 10,000 times."

HOW TO PRACTICE >>

- Create a practice schedule that includes the skills you need to improve as well as those you already do well.
- Ask your coaches to provide suggestions for which skills to practice.
- Work on the same skills your coaches emphasize during team practices.
- Concentrate on each activity performed during practice.

SAMPLE PRACTICE SESSION >>

- Warm up and stretch
- Drill 1
- Drill 2
- Drill 3
- Cool down and stretch

NOTE >> It is common for youth athletes to feel frustrated or want to quit while trying to master a technique. However, they will see improvement with regular practice and learn how to overcome adversity to achieve goals, a skill that will help them in all areas of life.

ATHLETES >> Great baseball players always find ways to practice baseball when they are away from the field. There are even ways to relax while still improving your skills.

To work on ball control and ball spin, I used to lie on my back on the floor and try to throw the ball up in front of me, seeing how close I could get to the ceiling without hitting it, and then letting it come back to me, then when I would catch it, I would try to change the grip as fast as I could to a four seam grip. I still do this to relax. I also did something similar outside. I would take a baseball or a tennis ball and throw it above a tree branch, trying to get it to come down without hitting the branch. I would even do this when I walked to school. Whenever I would see a good branch, I would throw the ball over it and try to catch it.

It's all about finding creative ways to incorporate games that build skills. There was a wall in my parents' garage where I would throw tennis balls to work on ground balls with either my glove or my bare hands. I would pretend that I was my favorite pitcher, Orel Hershiser, and try to hit small batter's box shapes on the garage wall. Sometimes, I would pretend I was Ozzie Smith turning double plays off the rebound of that same wall. This helped build hand-eye coordination and reinforced what I learned in practices.

PARENTS » The best athletes are the ones who ask what they can do outside of practice. The best parents are the ones who go outside and participate with them, even if just helping to put a ball on a tee or push record on their son's phone so he can watch the video later. The coaches give the team homework and tell them to work on certain things, but this may be too general and lack the specific work your child needs.

For example, a team may have trouble holding runners, so the coach asks players to work on this on their own.

However, if you're an outfielder, you might need to work on other things such as cutoff throws. The better athletes usually ask more questions and will use their phones to jot things down. For Little League players who might not have cell phones, parents can play a big role by writing notes or creating folders or logs on their phones. This way they can remember skills their kid excels in and those he needs to work on.

This kind of homework doesn't need to be long. It could be something simple—finding cue words to rely on when the kid struggles or going over something that has helped him have a good game. Over time, this kind of individualized homework can provide a lot of information to help a player improve.

I had a parent once text me that her son was really struggling in his first year of college, and she was worried about him. Later, while going through her phone, she came across an old folder that was titled "Pitching Lessons with Dave" and decided to send it to him.

He texted his mom about a week later after his best two games in a row, and she asked what changed. "Mom, you know that folder you sent me from my Little League pitching lessons?" he said. "It reminded me of some things I used to work on with Dave all the time. It was exactly what I was missing."

That kind of reminder can work wonders. Even today, I remember things my pitching coach Frank Pastore taught me 30 years ago. You never know what will help when you need it.

COACHES >> At Level 1, it's important to bring in games with practice. We used to play "Three Flies Up," which is a simple game of throwing a ball up in the air while three or four kids try to catch it. We did this before practice, which helped encourage kids to arrive early and have fun. We also played "Pickle," in which two guys have the ball and a couple of others are in the middle trying to get from one base to the other without getting tagged out. Another game involved throwing the ball against the wall. If a player tried to catch it and missed, he would have to run and touch the wall before someone else threw the ball on the wall.

All of these games are more fun than relying solely on one or two practices every week where the coach is telling players what to do. Don't think they are a waste of time either; they can even be valuable for team building. I still see old friends, and we talk about those times before practice and how much fun our coach was for allowing those games. Playing games in practice offers a nice balance between fun and improving skills.

NUTRITION

Nutrition plays a key role in athletic performance. Youth athletes are building muscle, burning calories, and growing. They need to eat and drink regularly to make up for calories they are burning and fluids they are using during practice and actual games.

An active youth baseball player needs to consume healthy food and beverages to help him with the following:

- Replenishing his energy supply
- Maintaining hydration
- Obtaining the vitamins and minerals needed to support metabolism, tissue growth, and repair
- Preventing injuries and/or illnesses
- Performing at his best both on and off the field

NOTE >> All of the **COMPLETE ATHLETE** sports nutrition guidelines provided by Courtney M. Sullivan, founder of Nutrition for Body and Mind. Sullivan is a Registered Dietitian certified by the Academy of Nutrition and Dietetics and a Certified Personal Trainer certified by the National Academy of Sports Medicine. At the end of this manual are more detailed guidelines as well as suggested meals and recipes developed by Sullivan.

GENERAL SPORTS NUTRITION GUIDELINES >>

- All athletes should consume five or more balanced meals spread throughout the day, every 3 to 4 hours.
- Meals should be eaten 2 to 3 hours before practice or games, and snacks eaten 1 to 1.5 hours before practice or games.

- Eat when you're hungry to prevent lean-muscle breakdown; stop when you're full to prevent being sluggish.
- Eat breakfast within 30 minutes of waking to prevent lean-muscle breakdown, increase energy and concentration, and maintain good blood-sugar control.
- Choose whole grains, fresh fruit, and lean protein for breakfast.
- Eat well-balanced meals and snacks consisting of carbohydrates, lean proteins, and heart-healthy fats.
- Drink a protein shake or eat a snack or meal that has equal amounts protein and carbohydrates within 30 minutes of a workout.
- Choose fresh, whole foods whenever possible (instead of processed foods that are packaged or refined) to increase nutritional value. Avoid foods that are high in sugar and/or trans fat.

LEVEL-1 ATHLETE NUTRITION GUIDELINES »

Each individual has different macronutrient needs, based on height, weight, age, activity level, and genetic background. The following macronutrient guidelines are based on age and estimated activity level for a Level 1 athlete:

- 60 percent carbohydrate
- 15 percent protein
- 25 percent fat
- No more than 7 percent saturated fat
- No trans fat
- 25 grams of fiber per day
- No more than 150 calories per day from sugar (37.5 grams or 9 teaspoons)

To fulfill these macronutrient needs, choose from the following:

CARBOHYDRATES High-fiber foods, such as whole-grain bread, brown rice, whole-grain pasta (or gluten-free versions), beans, starchy vegetables (e.g., corn, peas, potatoes), quinoa, and cereal

PROTEINS Chicken, turkey, or fish, especially wild salmon, tuna, trout, mackerel, and sardines, which are high in heart-healthy omega-3 fatty acids

FATS Low-fat cheese, nuts/nut butters (natural peanut butter or almond butter), avocado, seeds, and heart-healthy oils such as extra-virgin olive oil, canola oil, grapeseed oil, and flaxseed oil

VEGETABLES Preferably leafy green vegetables

PARENTS >> Before tournaments or big games, parents should prepare something that's going to give the athlete fuel and energy instead of just filling his stomach. Baseball tournaments usually have a snack counter or barbecue pit with greasy, fatty food. The kids might crave that, but food is fuel—especially when you're in the middle of a baseball tournament with two or three games a day. We need to give kids the right nutrition, including simple snacks such as oranges and fruits.

There are plenty of recommendations in this book on foods that provide optimal energy that lasts throughout the day. Too often, we see kids fade in late innings or not play as well as they did at the start of a tournament because they didn't eat nutritious food. Better nutrition gives our kids an edge as the season progresses.

A coach of ours runs a travel ball team with young athletes and one year had a successful summer, winning more than his share of tournaments. This coach isn't known for aggressively recruiting top players from faraway cities to create super teams, so his success was a little surprising to some outside of their program.

I asked him what made such a huge difference. He said he made it a priority to have a meeting specifically for the parents who wanted to learn more about eating well and how it would benefit their athletes for the season and foster long-term healthy habits. He brought in a local nutritionist, and she answered questions and even brought in sample food boxes of healthy options for parents to bring to the field or serve after tournaments and practices. They were impressed by the coach's effort, and the team really rallied around the idea and followed the plan.

This coach said he used to watch the other teams' parents sprint with their kids between games to try and be first in line at local fast-food places, worrying about getting back in time for the game or anxious because they were waiting 30 minutes for a burrito. Meanwhile, his players were all sitting together in the shade eating their boxed lunches and eating FUEL instead of junk.

JOIN THE CONVERSATION!

Live your sport & join the **COMPLETE ATHLETE** community of athletes, parents, and coaches by downloading the app today!

HYDRATION

All athletes need to drink water before, during, and after practices and games. This is especially important on days when both temperatures and humidity levels are high. If a youth baseball player does not drink enough water, he could suffer from dehydration. Warning signs of dehydration include the following:

- Thirst
- Irritability
- Headaches
- Weakness
- Dizziness
- Cramps
- Nausea
- Increased risk of injury

HOW TO MAINTAIN PROPER HYDRATION* >>

- Before exercise, drink 16 to 20 full ounces within the two-hour period prior to exercise.
- During exercise, drink 4 to 6 full ounces.
- After exercise, replace 24 full ounces for every 1 pound of body weight lost during exercise.

RECOVERY

Youth baseball players need to eat and drink within 30 minutes of a practice or game to make up for calories they are burning and fluids they are using. Replenishing calories and fluids also aids in muscle **RECOVERY** and repair.

---

* Adapted from guidelines provided by the American College of Sports Medicine (ACSM)

HOW TO REPLENISH CALORIES AND FLUIDS »

- Drink 24 ounces of fluid for every pound of sweat lost within two hours of a game or practice.
- Consume 5 to 10 grams of protein plus an equal amount of carbohydrates within the 30-minute recovery window.

SLEEP »

Just as increased activity creates a greater need for calories, it also creates a greater need for sleep. Recovery also refers to allowing the body to rest and heal from the demands of practices and games.

According to the National Sleep Foundation, a Level 1 youth athlete should get 10 to 11 hours of sleep each night for proper growth and development. If that's not possible or he needs additional recovery time, he can take short naps (no more than 30 minutes) or engage in quiet rest periods (lying down, reading, or watching TV).

PARENTS » When I played Little League baseball, I was on the All-Star team representing our league. We practiced every single day for two weeks straight and had a ton of confidence. The night before the first day of the tournament, we had a small kickoff party, and six or seven of us had a sleepover. We were so excited about the tournament and how well we expected to do that we stayed up late.

The next day, we were so tired and ran out of gas early. We ended up losing the first game of the tournament, which put us in the losers bracket where we had to win every game or go home. After that loss, our coach told us, "Time to sleep in your own beds."

The night before games, it's important that players do not stay up late hanging out with friends or playing video games. Our coach was right to demand we follow our normal routines. That was a big help, and we won the rest of the games and went on to the state tournament. We still hung out and bonded, choosing team breakfasts or, on a day off, going to a movie, rather than having sleepover parties. Proper sleep became an important part of that great run.

MENTALITY

Being a better athlete does not necessarily mean training only your body; you must also spend time training your mind. Certainly, a youth baseball player must spend time physically preparing his body to meet the demands of a practice session or game. Similarly, engaging in mental preparation can help him perform at a higher level by creating the proper mind-set for either practice or a game.

At Level 1, a youth baseball player should be playing for the love of the game. While he may possess a competitive spirit and want to win, he should always remember that he is there to have fun.

NOTE >> If baseball is not fun for a youth baseball player, he probably will not achieve higher levels of performance. Likewise, if he's playing baseball simply because his parents want him to participate in a sport, not because he actually enjoys the game, he may not continue playing at higher levels of competition.

HOW TO MENTALLY PREPARE TO PLAY
OR PRACTICE BASEBALL »

- Take a few minutes to think about the game or practice you're about to engage in.
- Close your eyes and take a few deep breaths. As you slowly breathe in and out, picture yourself breathing in the fresh air as you run around the field.
- As you close your eyes allow yourself to hear all the noises around you, e.g. birds, wind, cars driving, kids playing, airplane passing by. Teach the mind to relax and observe.
- Think about your friends on the team and try to remember something funny or nice they recently said to you.
- Think about how much you like your teammates and respect your coaches. Promise to yourself that you will play your best for them—and for yourself.

PARENTS » Parents can offer a nice, quick cue to get the athlete into the right mindset before a game or practice without being too overbearing. We ask our kids what's the one thing they take from practice that they will work on in the coming week. I tell parents before they drop their kids off for practice or games to ask what they will work on or try to improve. The kids will answer "I'm going to keep my glove in the right position" or "I'm going to catch the ball with two hands" or "I'm going to hit the ball to right field." We ask the parents to try not to correct the kids. Let them say whatever they want and have fun with it. Make the way you ask as important as what you are asking. Ask with a smile, make it quick, and be excited to hear how it went afterward. Think of this in the same way as when you would pick your kids up from kindergarten and couldn't wait to hear what they had learned. Keep it simple.

We had a player who was only 9, but his father gave him too many things to think about. This dad consistently pointed out all the negatives, focusing on things his son needed to improve instead of reinforcing the positive.

One time, the kid was on the verge of tears when he arrived. We asked him what was wrong. He told us that his dad had yelled at him in the parking lot, telling him, "You didn't work on this; you didn't work on that. You need to get better because I'm paying for your lessons." When the kid arrived, he was already broken. His mentality wasn't there, and he had one of the worst sessions he had ever had. The whole time we tried to get his spirits back up, but the damage had already been done by his father making it too hard.

1.3 FITNESS

FITNESS matters. A baseball player needs to develop strength and speed to play the game effectively and prevent injuries. He also needs a high degree of mobility. Mobility is the ability to move through a full range of motion. A **COMPLETE ATHLETE** maintains a high degree of the following:

LOWER-BODY STRENGTH

UPPER-BODY STRENGTH

FLEXIBILITY / MOBILITY

CORE STRENGTH

SPEED / QUICKNESS / ENDURANCE

DANIEL ROBERTSON >> *In sixth grade, I found my own personal trainer. Even then, I knew I loved to work out and had to stay fit to play baseball. In junior high, I tore my ACL, which was a big shock. I knew I had to work hard in rehab to get it better and play again. That injury taught me to work hard and was also a powerful reminder of what I would have to do to meet my ultimate goal of playing professional baseball.*

LOWER-BODY STRENGTH

LOWER-BODY STRENGTH is necessary for nearly any athletic activity. In baseball, a great deal of power and torque for hitting and throwing comes from the lower body. Lower-body muscles include large, powerful muscles—quads, glutes, hamstrings, and calves—as well as smaller muscles located in and around ankle, hip, and knee joints. All play major roles in producing health and power. Strength in these areas will give a Level 1 athlete the advantage of being more athletic and coordinated than the competition.

Exercises such as single-leg wall sits and broad jumps can help a youth baseball player develop the leg strength, posture, and balance needed to compete at higher levels. Single-leg squats (which come in higher levels) and single-leg wall sits also can help determine if one leg is stronger than the other and can be used to develop a better balance of strength in both legs.

TO PEFORM A SINGLE-LEG WALL SIT >>

- Stand with your back against a smooth wall, feet approximately shoulder-width apart.
- Slowly slide your back down the wall until both knees and hips are at a 90-degree angle.
- Lift one foot off the ground and hold it as long as possible. After a period of rest, lift the other foot and hold it.

NOTE >> If you can hold one foot up considerably longer than the other, you may need to work on developing a better balance of strength in both legs.

TO PEFORM A BROAD JUMP »

- Stand behind a line marked on the ground, feet
  slightly apart.
- Use a two-foot takeoff and landing, swinging the arms
  and bending the knees to provide forward drive.
- Jump as far as possible, landing on both feet without
  falling backward.

UPPER-BODY STRENGTH

UPPER-BODY STRENGTH is also important for baseball
although maybe not the first thing you think of at this age.
Many people still believe lifting weights can be bad for
your health, stunt growth, or even cause you to get bulky.
Studies have repeatedly shown the complete opposite of
this, and proper strength training actually can help keep
you from getting sick as often and promote healthier
habits. At each level, we will test your ability to lift your
body weight in exercises such as the common push-up
and pull-up. We will also test your upper-body strength by
throwing a small medicine ball.

UPPER-BODY STRENGTH IS DEVELOPED
IN TWO DISTINCT WAYS »

PULL EXERCISES in which you are pulling something
toward your body, help increase upper back strength and
mobility. The flexed-arm hang (also called bent-arm hold)
is just one type of pull exercise.

PUSH EXERCISES in which you are pushing something
away from your body, are great for increasing strength
and mobility in the chest and arms.

Some of the best upper-body push exercises are body-weight exercises such as push-ups. Bear in mind that bigger is not necessarily better. In fact, bulky upper-body muscles can actually decrease mobility.

TO PERFORM A FLEXED-ARM HANG >>

- Grasp an overhead bar using an underhand grip (palms facing toward body).
- Position the body with arms flexed and the chin clearing the bar. The chest should be held close to the bar, legs hanging straight.
- Hold this position as long as possible.

TO PERFORM PUSH-UPS >>

- Lie facedown on the floor (or mat) with hands under the shoulders or slightly wider than the chest, fingers straight, legs straight and parallel.
- Straighten the arms, pushing the upper-body up and keeping the back and knees straight.
- Bend the arms to lower the upper-body until the elbows are at a 90-degree angle and the upper arms are parallel to the floor.
- Perform as many repetitions as possible without resting.

ROTATIONAL MEDICINE BALL THROWS >>

Follow the same motor pattern used in games. They help to teach youth baseball players how to transfer power from rotational movements such as swinging and throwing. It may be the single most important component in training to hit and throw harder.

TO PERFORM A ROTATIONAL MEDICINE BALL THROW

- Stand perpendicular to a start line (such as in a pitching or hitting stance).
- Hold a medicine ball in both hands, placing back hand on the back of the ball and the front hand under the ball.
- Draw the ball back with only a slight bend at the elbows, keeping the ball between the waist and chest.
- In one swift motion, fling the ball up and forward (optimally at a 45-degree angle).

FLEXIBILITY / MOBILITY

A good degree of **FLEXIBILITY** and **MOBILITY** leads to better baseball technique and helps to prevent injuries.

The sit-and-reach test is used to assess and improve a youth athlete's level of lower-body flexibility and mobility. The shoulder-stretch test is used to assess and improve a youth athlete's level of upper-body flexibility and mobility.

TO PERFORM THE SIT-AND-REACH TEST >>

NOTE >> You'll need a box that is 12 inches high, such as a milk crate. Tape a yardstick or ruler to the top so that the first 9 inches hang over the edge and the 9-inch mark is exactly on the edge against which you will place your feet.

- Place the box against a wall.
- Sit on the floor in front of the box with your legs straight in front of you and the soles of your feet flat against the front side of the box. (The overhanging part of the ruler should be pointed at your chest or midsection.)

- Keeping the legs straight and flat on the floor, stretch forward and reach along the ruler with one hand on top of the other, palms down.
- Stretch forward three times without bouncing; then reach as far as possible, holding at the farthest point for at least three seconds.

TO PERFORM THE SHOULDER-STRETCH TEST >>

- Stand with feet slightly apart.
- Place one hand behind the head and back over the shoulder with the palm touching your body and fingers directed downward.
- Place the other arm behind your back, palm facing outward and fingers upward.
- Reach as far as possible, attempting to touch the fingers of each hand together.
- Repeat with the other side.

CORE STRENGTH

Core muscles provide power and stability for a lot of baseball movements, including throwing a ball, swinging a bat, and running the bases. The core is what transfers power from a rotational movement such as swinging and throwing. The core muscles are located in the abdominal area and lower back and glutes.

While sit-ups and crunches can be useful for strengthening the abdominal muscles, they're not the most effective exercises for strengthening the core. The plank is one of the most effective core workouts.

TO PERFORM A PLANK >>

- Get down on the floor with your hands apart slightly wider than shoulder-width, your arms straight and supporting your weight.
- Make sure your body stays straight. Your hips shouldn't be sticking way up in the air or sagging.
- Hold that position as long as you can.

TO PERFORM A SIDE PLANK >>

- Lie on your side with your legs straight.
- Prop up your upper-body on your elbow and forearm.
- Make sure your elbow is aligned with the shoulder.
- Brace your core by contracting your abs forcefully, and then raise your hips until your body forms a straight line from your ankles to your shoulders.
- Breathe deeply while holding this position.
- Repeat this exercise on your other side.

The **HIP-LIFT MARCH** helps to measure—and improve— the strength and endurance of the back muscles.

TO PERFORM A HIP-LIFT MARCH >>

- Lie flat on your back, knees bent 90 degrees and feet flat on the ground.
- Lift hips as high as possible; only shoulders and feet should touch the ground.
- Keeping hips at the same height, lift each knee in a controlled marching motion for as long as possible.

SPEED / QUICKNESS / ENDURANCE

THERE ARE TWO TYPES OF BASEBALL SPEED »

- Straightaway speed on the base paths or in the outfield.
- Lateral (side-to-side) quickness, such as when an
  infielder moves to get a ground ball.

The 30-yard sprint helps an athlete improve straightaway
speed. The 5-10-5 Shuttle Run, or Pro Agility Drill, is a
great way to improve lateral quickness because it helps to
hone an athlete's ability to accelerate, decelerate, stop,
and reaccelerate without losing balance. The Beep Test is
a good way to measure and improve endurance.

TO PERFORM A 5-10-5 SHUTTLE RUN »

- Set up three marker cones 5 yards apart.
- Start at the middle marker cone in a three-point stance.

- Turn and run 5 yards to the right side and touch the marker cone with the right hand.
- Turn around and run 10 yards to the left and touch the marker cone with the left hand.
- Turn and finish by running back to the middle marker cone.

TO PERFORM A 30-YARD SPRINT »

- Place two cones 30 yards apart.
- Starting at one cone, run as fast as you can to the other cone.

TO PERFORM A BEEP TEST »

NOTE » You'll first need to download a Beep Test audio recording or Beep Test app, which will play beeps at set intervals. As the test proceeds, the interval between each successive beep reduces, forcing the athlete to increase his speed.

- Draw two lines 20 yards apart.
- Stand behind one of the lines, face the second line, and begin running when instructed by the recording.
- Continue running between the two lines, turning when signaled by the recorded beeps. After about one minute, a sound indicates an increase in speed, and the beeps will be closer together.
- The test is stopped when the athlete can no longer keep in sync with the recording.

JOIN THE CONVERSATION!

For additional drills to improve speed, mobility, and agility, be sure to check out the **COMPLETE ATHLETE** app. New video content is continually updated!

LEVEL-1 FITNESS TEST

LOWER-BODY STRENGTH
- Single-leg wall sit of 30 seconds on each leg
- Broad jump of 65 inches or greater

UPPER-BODY STRENGTH
- Flexed-arm hang of 15 seconds
- 20 push-ups in 60 seconds
- Rotational medicine ball throw of at least 20 feet with an 8-pound ball

FLEXIBILITY/MOBILITY
- At least 29 centimeters in the sit-and-reach test
- Shoulder-stretch test (pass or fail)

CORE STRENGTH
- 2.5-minute plank
- 30-second side plank on each side
- Hip-lift march with perfect form for 60 seconds
- Balance 30 seconds on each leg

SPEED/QUICKNESS/ENDURANCE
- 5-10-5 Shuttle Run in 5.6 seconds
- 30-yard sprint in 5 seconds
- 8 Beep Test minimum score of Level 6

1.4 TECHNIQUE

In just about any sport, the basic **TECHNIQUES** are the most important skills to master. These skills are the building blocks upon which more advanced skills are learned. As a youth athlete achieves higher levels of success in baseball, he will begin to specialize in a particular position on the team.

A **COMPLETE ATHLETE** not only masters the basic and advanced skills needed to play the game of baseball but also understands the roles and responsibilities of every position on a team and how all the positions work together to win games. There are five basic skills of baseball:

THROWING

HITTING

INFIELD FIELDING

OUTFIELD FIELDING

GAME ASSESSMENT

THROWING

THROWING the baseball is required for every position on the field. Good throwing technique requires accuracy, arm strength, and proper mechanics to make plays. Your ultimate goal is to mimic the habits and technique of high-level infielders. Infielders are able to play any position on the field due to their efficient arm path and mechanics.

NOTE >> I highly recommend learning the shortstop or catching position while playing youth baseball. This may not be the position you play on your team or in games, but it will help you establish great habits, which will help when you start to specialize in a certain position. Spend some time each week taking ground balls and throwing from the shortstop position to all bases. The short, quick arm action of shortstops and catchers will make transitioning to any other position much easier. (Practicing catching may also help eliminate any fear of being hit by the baseball.) You may need to do this on your own or outside practice if your coach doesn't have time.

TECHNICAL TIPS >>

- Keep your body under control and your eyes on the target.
- The gloved side shoulder should be slightly higher on break than the front shoulder, the palm of the glove facing toward the target, elbows bent 90 degree angles, try not to lock out elbows and get long.
- Throw the ball with a smooth, fluid motion, bringing the ball out of the glove, thumb down, and making a short compact arm path in a rhythmic circle. Accelerate when the elbow is higher than the shoulder.
- As the throw is completed, the glove should be at shoulder height, near your chest, and facing toward the player. Your posture should be balanced, good follow through and slightly tall as if you had to immediately catch a ball thrown back to you.

COMMON MISTAKES >>

- Rushing your throws
- Max effort throws that cause poor mechanics
- Throwing off-balance

- Head and glove pulling off
- Stabbing as you take the ball out of glove
- Getting your arm path too long
- Body collapsing right before ball release

MLB PITCHER >> *What you learn in Little League might pay off down the road. I turned to the knuckleball out of desperation to save my professional career. I was at an impasse, trying to move up the minor league ladder, when I decided to incorporate it into my pitching. That's a pitch you never master. I started throwing it when I was 9 and used it as trick pitch over the years. In 2010, the Indians saw me messing with it and told me to use it as an out pitch. By 2011, it was my only pitch. Learning it all those years ago and keeping up with the skills to make it relevant certainly came in handy.*

HITTING

HITTING in baseball requires a great deal of practice: first, to simply make contact with the baseball using the bat, and second, to be able to hit the ball with a degree of power/accuracy.

When preparing to hit the ball, move your body into a proper starting position with more of your weight on the back foot. Hands and upper-body should be in a relaxed, comfortable position not too far from your body. Eyes and head are focused on pitcher. Blink your eyes before pitcher starts his motion to clear your mind and focus.

When attempting to hit the ball, attack down toward the ball and allow your momentum to go toward the pitcher. Finishing your swing with a slight upper arc as you hit the ball with backspin and fully extend your arms.

TECHNICAL TIPS >>

- Choose a batting stance that suits you.
- Less movement in your body equals more consistent swings.
- If popping the ball up is a problem, try keeping the front shoulder closed and head on the ball longer.
- If hitting the ball too much on the ground is a problem, stay back on the rear foot a little longer.

COMMON MISTAKES >>

- Getting too anxious
- Allowing the swing to become long
- Not maintaining good form throughout
- Swinging at non-strikes

INFIELD FIELDING

INFIELD FIELDING refers to catching balls in the infield. Infielders should be able to catch balls with either their backhand or forehand and while moving. There are two types of catching techniques to master for Level 1:

- Catching ground balls
- Catching pop flies

TECHNICAL TIPS TO PROPERLY CATCH A GROUND BALL >>

- Stay calm and relaxed, but be ready for the ball before it is hit.
- Use your knees, not your waist, to lower yourself to the ground.

- Ensure the glove is in contact with the ground when attempting to make a play.
- Catch the ball cleanly in the web of the glove, not the pocket.

TECHNICAL TIPS TO PROPERLY CATCH A BALL IN THE AIR >>

- Stay calm and relaxed, but be ready for the ball before it is hit.
- Keep your glove in front of your face above eye level when the ball is in the air.
- Position your body so the ball is in front of the point of catch, ready to throw the ball after catch.
- Keep an eye on the ball as it moves through the air and see the ball into the glove.

COMMON MISTAKES >>

- Being afraid of the ball
- Not having the glove in good fielding position
- Not being ready or being flat-footed
- Arriving late to your fielding position

OUTFIELD FIELDING

The main activity in **OUTFIELD FIELDING** is catching fly balls and throwing them to the infield/cutoff man. An outfielder must be able to catch while running to the left, to the right, backward, and forward. He must also be able to throw the ball quickly and accurately. Outfielders must also know when and where to back up outfielders, bases, or infield hits that their teammates can't catch.

TECHNICAL TIPS TO PROPERLY CATCH A BALL »

- Stay calm and relaxed, but be ready for the ball before it is hit.
- Anticipate where balls will be hit or where you may need to go after ball the is in play.
- Keep your glove in front of your face above eye level when you are in position to catch the ball.
- Keep an eye on the ball as it moves through the air and see the ball into the glove.
- Keep ground balls in front of you.

COMMON MISTAKES »

- Being afraid of the ball
- Not knowing situations pre-pitch
- Not having the glove in good fielding position
- Not being ready or being flat-footed
- Arriving late to your fielding position

GAME ASSESSMENT

GAME ASSESSMENT refers to the ability to perform the above techniques during the demands of an actual game, not just in practice. It also includes developing good judgment regarding in-game decisions. Game assessment involves the following:

- Making accurate throws
- Fielding your position properly
- Making good contact off live pitches
- Making smart base-running decisions
- When pitching, throwing strikes at least 60 percent of the time

- Backing up other outfielders and bases
- Anticipating where the ball may be hit by knowing what pitch is being thrown (and what the hitter may do with it)
- Hitting your cutoff man 100 percent of the time

COMMON MISTAKES »

- Not remaining fully focused before every pitch
- Making poor decisions
- When pitching, making poor pitch choices or avoiding contact
- Forgetting to back up bases

JOIN THE CONVERSATION!

Sports performance is also influenced by preparation and proper mentality before games. Learn more by downloading the **COMPLETE ATHLETE** app.

LEVEL-1 SKILLS TEST

To pass Level 1 Technique, a youth baseball player must be able to perform the following:

THROWING »

- Throw the baseball accurately to another person 10 times in a row from a distance of at least 60 feet.
- Proper form, including balance and glove-side control, must be displayed at all times.
- Demonstrate arm strength by throwing the ball at least 100 feet five times consecutively. Must use good mechanics and hit the target within a 6-foot radius.

HITTING »

- Using good mechanics, make solid contact in a controlled format such as off the tee, front toss, or overhand toss from a coach.
- Make hard contact off the tee 10 times in a row. At least five should be line drives (i.e., the ball doesn't hit the ground until after it has passed the pitcher).
- Make hard contact off underhand soft toss five times consecutively.

- Make hard contact off an overhand toss by the coach five times consecutively.

INFIELD FIELDING »

- Catch 10 ground balls in a row thrown from a coach, alternating from forehand to backhand while running forward and straight at them.

NOTE » Cones can be set up 10 yards apart, the fielder in the middle and the coach throwing toward the cones for backhand and forehand practice.

- Catch 10 ground balls in a row hit off the bat.

NOTE » Allow player 5 seconds after each catch to reset.

- Cleanly field five grounders and quickly exchange the ball out of the glove using proper throwing technique.

OUTFIELD FIELDING »

- Catch fly balls 10 times in a row thrown to you from coach.

NOTE » Set up a 15-yard-radius circle in the outfield.

- Stand in a ready position in the center. Have the coach throw one ball at a time to alternating areas of the circle. Once the ball is caught, allow player 10 seconds to reset.
- Catch the ball five times in a row, hit to you off the bat.

NOTE » Balls should be hit with height and require the outfielder to move and catch them while running or set up properly to catch a fly ball.

- While running, catch a ball thrown from a coach five times consecutively.

NOTE >> The balls should be thrown to resemble a line drive, with two balls thrown left/back, two balls thrown to the right/back, and one thrown forward. Catches should be made running in both directions without losing stride.

- Cleanly field five grounders and quickly exchange the ball out of the glove using proper throwing technique.

To pass **LEVEL 1 GAME ASSESSMENT**, a youth athlete must have a coach assess him in these six areas:

- Accuracy
- Proper fielding
- Making smart base-running decisions
- Backing up other outfielders and bases
- Remaining fully focused before every pitch
- Understanding different pitching strategies and what the hitter may do based on the pitch thrown

1.5 LIFESTYLE

As youth baseball players achieve higher levels of success, they will find the demands on their time increasing. Creating a healthy balance between sports, academics, family obligations, and social activities requires strong time-management skills and a clear understanding of what's important.

A **COMPLETE ATHLETE** prioritizes the various elements of his life as follows:

FAMILY

ACADEMICS

SOCIAL LIFE

ROLE MODEL

LIVING YOUR SPORT

FAMILY

Parents play a number of important roles in the lives of youth baseball players: At Level 1, parents serve three main roles.

- Chauffeur, by driving to and from practices and games.
- Financier, by paying for equipment, uniforms, team snacks, and more.
- Cheerleader and spectator, by taking time out of their busy schedules to attend games and cheer on their children.

Youth baseball players sometimes feel that baseball is the most important part of their lives. They believe that everyone should drop everything to accommodate their sports activities. They need to remember that baseball may not be the most important part of their parents' lives. After all, parents have other responsibilities such as jobs, other children, possibly their own parents, and themselves.

Youth baseball players must remember to show appreciation for all the things their parents do to support them as they move up the levels of play. They do this by not seeking to be the center of attention and finding ways to help out their parents.

DO YOU ACT AS THOUGH YOU'RE THE CENTER OF ATTENTION?

Are your parents often stressed out because you've made a big deal out of a small situation? Do you insist your parents buy you the newest generation of bats after going 0–4, or a brand new $400 glove after an error? Do you tell them, "It's not me; it's my equipment." Do you often forget your glove at the field and have them ask your coaches if they have seen it? Do you ever throw a fit when you have to go support your sister or brother at their games? Do you forget to tell your parents about a change in practice time?

If these are common occurrences for you, you need to make some changes. You need to open your eyes and start paying attention to the needs of others. For example, if you do forget a glove, bat, or jacket at practice, then you need to ask your parents if you can use their phone to call—not text—the coach and ask if he picked up your lost item. If your coach schedules a special practice on a Tuesday afternoon and it conflicts with your mom's schedule, as she has to take your sister to her regular practice, arrange to get a ride with a teammate.

PARENTS >> I was at a park with my 5-year-old daughter, and she noticed a baseball practice going on. She wanted to watch so I could explain baseball to her a little.

We went over and sat in the stands, and it didn't take long to see that one of the players really stood out. He was playing shortstop, and he caught everything hit at him and threw the ball across the diamond on a line. When he came up to the plate to hit, I couldn't wait to see him swing. This boy had clean, new gear, and his uniform (batting gloves, wrist bands, and a new helmet) looked perfect; the other players were still in their school clothes.

While he looked the part, things quickly turned ugly. When the volunteer coach missed a few times for perfect pitches, the kid pounded his bat on the home plate and put his hand out to show where to put the ball. He even yelled, "Throw a strike!" The poor coach, who was still wearing his work clothes (a mechanic's shirt with his name tag on it), was doing his best. He wasn't a professional athlete, but he was working hard and giving his time for these kids.

After a few good pitches and some bad ones, the kid threw his bat and walked over to the stands where only one parent was standing up. It was his dad, and he looked frustrated with the pitching as well. The dad even turned his back and put his hands up just like his son. They both showed the same arrogance. Like father, like son.

I couldn't believe the missed opportunity by the dad to turn the situation into a learning moment. He should have told his child this was embarrassing and unacceptable behavior—you *never* show up coaches who are doing their best. The dad could have explained that, and they could have then practiced more swings once they were home. The father also could have reminded the son that it's good practice to be patient at the plate and wait for your pitch. If this kid learned to be humble and a good sport, he would be the kind of player everyone would want to be around and have on their team. As it was, if I had been coaching, I would have actively *avoided* putting him on my team. Talent does not trump attitude.

LOOK FOR WAYS TO HELP PARENTS WHEN POSSIBLE >>

Your parents devote an enormous amount of their time taking you to and from games and practices, buying your equipment, watching you play, and cheering for you. When they get home, they have many responsibilities waiting for them, including cooking meals, cleaning the house, doing laundry, and helping with homework.

When you take on a few chores, such as keeping your room clean or doing the dishes after dinner, you're taking some of the burden off your parents' shoulders and, at the same time, showing gratitude for all they do for you.

DANIEL ROBERTSON >> *My parents were always in my corner. They were a big influence, always pushing me and knowing how much I loved the game. They encouraged me to work hard in the cage and the field and to get in the gym. They instilled a good work ethic in me at a young age, which helped me get where I am.*

ACADEMICS

Many youth baseball players (and many parents as well) have the misconception that if an athlete is good enough, grades don't matter. Nothing could be further from the truth. For one thing, college coaches know that athletes who perform well in school, as well as on the field, are generally mature individuals with good time-management skills. These are the student-athletes coaches want in their programs.

As a youth baseball player travels the path toward becoming a **COMPLETE ATHLETE**, he must develop a lifestyle that allows him to maintain good grades. Granted, not everyone is going to be an A+ student, but a few key strategies can go a long way toward improving grades.

STRATEGIES FOR MAINTAINING GOOD GRADES »

HAND IN ALL ASSIGNMENTS ON TIME. Many teachers give full credit for homework turned in on time.

BE ORGANIZED. Having all materials organized can help you complete your assignments on time.

PAY CLOSE ATTENTION IN CLASS. Focus on what the teacher is saying, take good notes, and follow directions.

STUDY A LITTLE BIT EVERY DAY. Just as practicing drills can help improve your baseball skills, regular study time helps you better retain information.

ASK QUESTIONS. Your teachers want you to succeed. If you're having trouble with the material, your teacher is the first person you should go to for help.

DON'T CRAM FOR TESTS. Put in extra study time at least a few days before the exam. Read through textbook chapters, study your notes, and take any practice tests available to you.

BEHAVE APPROPRIATELY IN CLASS. Good behavior starts with knowing the rules. In school, the rules usually include sitting still at your desk, listening to your teacher, and raising your hand if you want to speak. Other schools may have other rules; however, knowing—and obeying—those rules generally leads to good behavior.

SOCIAL LIFE

A healthy **SOCIAL LIFE** is important for all young people, not just youth athletes. Friends provide companionship and recreation. Friends also give advice to one another and often help ease anxiety during times of stress. Young people who don't have friends tend to be lonely and unhappy and have lower levels of academic achievement and self-esteem.

While the social lives of many youth baseball players revolve around their teammates, many have friends outside of sports. Either way, a baseball player's lifestyle should include spending time with friends outside of baseball and learning to be considerate of those friends.

HOW TO MAKE FRIENDS OUTSIDE OF BASEBALL >>

There are many ways to make friends outside of baseball. You are surrounded by potential friends in school, in your neighborhood, and even at your church or temple. By opening your eyes and observing other kids, you can find mutual likes (or even dislikes) over which to bond.

For example, you may notice another kid wearing a jersey representing your favorite team. By saying to that person, "Hey, I like that team, too," you make a connection to a potential friend. Asking questions to get to know the other person can help create a true friendship.

HOW TO BE CONSIDERATE OF YOUR FRIENDS' TIME AND OBLIGATIONS >>

Whether you develop friendships with your teammates or your classmates, you need to remember that everyone has responsibilities. Other kids also have homework to do, sports or music to practice, siblings to babysit, and chores to complete.

Sometimes you'll make plans with a friend only to have him or her cancel at the last minute. It may be because they forgot about a family event, or their parents scheduled something and forgot to tell them about it. It may even be because they suddenly realized they needed more time to get a school assignment finished.

Whatever the reason, being considerate of your friends means not getting angry or throwing a fit when plans change or when they can't seem to find time to be with you. Be understanding and remember next time it might be you having to cancel at the last minute.

ROLE MODEL

A **ROLE MODEL** is someone who possesses qualities that others admire. They are the people others look up to and want to be like. Being a good role model is another attribute college and professional coaches like to see in the athletes they recruit.

Role models demonstrate respect for others and for themselves. To be a good role model, start by demonstrating respect for others in these ways:

• Listening carefully without interrupting or fidgeting when someone else is speaking
• Addressing people by their names
• Valuing other people's opinions
• Letting teammates know they are appreciated
• Refraining from insulting people, making fun of them, or talking about them behind their backs

COACH MIKE MARTIN >> *Parents need to understand that they are influencing their child every single day by their attitude, and the young man derives his attitude from his parents. If his parents are negative, undoubtedly, that young man is always going to find an excuse for why he didn't do well. I've seen it countless times: Positive parents raise positive children. Attitude is everything, and it starts when they are small.*

LIVING YOUR SPORT

Youth baseball players who are serious about getting a college scholarship and possibly playing baseball professionally are generally committed to practicing more and doing whatever they can to improve their skills and physical fitness. Many also cultivate a lifestyle in which they **LIVE THEIR SPORT.**

Some youth baseball players may never be seen without a ball in their hands. Others may spend time watching professional baseball games live or on television. Still, others may spend time reading about their favorite players to learn what they've done to succeed.

HOW TO LIVE YOUR SPORT >>

At Level 1, a youth baseball player begins to live his sport simply by playing for the love of the game. He should make it a priority to have fun and bond with other boys who share this love. Go enjoy an MLB game from the stands, get there when the gates open, and watch warmups and batting practice.

JOIN THE CONVERSATION!

Find more ways to live a balanced lifestyle in the **COMPLETE ATHLETE** app.

TREVOR HOFFMAN

The most important influence in any child's life is his or her parents, and that was absolutely the case for me. But in order to understand the character and wisdom of my mom and dad, it's important to give a little family history.

My mother was a professional ballerina in England; she met my father, a Marine veteran from World War II and a talented singer, when they were both part of the same touring company in Europe in the early 1950s.

They married and continued to tour for several years in the United States before moving to Southern California, where my mother focused on running our home with incredible economy and an eye toward not wasting anything or taking it for granted while my father continued working as a professional singer. Dad's voice was tremendous and he was in high demand—but that also meant that he was away a lot, working in Los Angeles or touring on the road.

One day, when my dad returned home from another long tour, my brother Greg (who was about 7), met him at the door and said, "Who are you?"

Dad retired from music on the spot, and the very next day he applied for a job at the local post office. He spent the next 30 years working for the postal service during the day, then coming home for supper and heading down to Anaheim to work as an usher at night for the Angels. He earned the nickname "The Singing Usher" because he not only belted out tunes to entertain the fans, but also would fill in singing the national anthem on occasion if the scheduled performer didn't show up.

My brothers, Greg and Glenn, are roughly 14 and 10 years older than me, respectively, so my dad's career change happened before I was even born, but I felt the effects of it. My reality was always a set of parents who were committed to being wholly present and invested in the lives of their family, and this has been the most powerful legacy they could have left my brothers and me.

They never pressured us to go into sports or to perform at a certain level, but they were always present to facilitate and encourage our passions. When they came to my games, Dad was careful to hang back and watch from a distance, at least at first, so that he was never tempted to become overly excited or inject himself in the game. It was the perfect balance of unwavering support and room to learn and grow as my own person. In fact, I adopted that same approach to watching my own three sons play.

We used to joke that it was like "Where's Waldo?" for the first few innings; they scanned the stands for me because they knew I was there, but I might be standing behind the bleachers or positioned near the concession stand—never anywhere obvious. I fought the urge to sit front and center because I wanted them to have the assurance that I was present, but not the pressure of feeling as though they had to perform for me.

My parents also shaped my perspective on life with the way that they responded to some of my early childhood health concerns. When I was six weeks old, I lost a kidney due to a blood clot, which meant that my participation in athletics was limited to low-contact sports; football, wrestling, and anything else that might pose a risk to my remaining kidney were off the table. My parents, however, made sure I never felt this as a loss or as a reason to feel sorry for myself. As I grew older, I was aware of other children who had lost kidneys due to cancer or an infection, and I quickly came to realize how lucky I was to still have one functioning kidney and that I was able to spend my afternoons on the playground instead of in dialysis. I knew Dad and Mom were concerned about me, but they also didn't treat me as though I was fragile or had to live my life packed in bubble wrap. They let me be a kid and encouraged me to participate in everything I was able to enjoy: baseball, basketball, and just messing around with my friends.

The example I had from watching my parents proved to be one of the most significant forces in shaping my entire life, and I know I am not unique in that. It is safe to say that just about every child is profoundly shaped by his or her family life, be it positive or negative, and this is the most important investment parents can make toward the future success of their child—in school, in sports, in a career, and in life in general. For children who don't have that kind of strong home life, coaches can stand in the role of parents by modeling good choices; giving encouragement; and offering acceptance, safety, and belonging. We all know how essential a strong foundation is for a child, but it can be easy to lose sight of what that really looks like.

Your child needs to be given freedom not only to make his own mistakes but also simply to figure out who he really is. He wants to know that there is someone in the stands or dugout who is his biggest fan, but he also wants to prove he can stand on his own two feet and know that support won't disappear if he has a bad day on the field. He will believe about himself what he sees his parents model; if they treat him as though he is fragile or needs to be babied, he will believe that he lacks the strength and ability to succeed, and those limitations will extend to his dreams. Be present, and be sure your child knows you are present—but don't be so present that you crowd out his individuality and chance to just be a kid.

JOIN THE CONVERSATION!

For advice from coaches and professional athletes, check out tips & techniques in the **COMPLETE ATHLETE** app.

IN LEVEL 2

A baseball player is starting to develop his own personality on and off the field. Foundational skills are being refined with dedicated practice, and new skills are being learned. Off the field, attitude, preparation, and lifestyle begin to play a larger role in preparing an athlete for higher levels. Mastering this level isn't just for athletes, though; coaches and parents will learn how to support players and appreciate the importance of balancing their involvement with encouraging their sons to reach their full potential.

2.1 ATTITUDE

A **POSITIVE ATTITUDE** is essential to an athlete's success both on and off the playing field, especially as he moves into higher levels of play. In fact, college coaches seek out athletes who display positive attitudes.

A positive attitude is something that can be developed with practice, just like any other skill. A **COMPLETE ATHLETE** makes a habit of demonstrating the following five attributes:

RESPECT

SPORTSMANSHIP

TEAMWORK

PROFESSIONALISM

LEADERSHIP

RESPECT

Showing **RESPECT** means treating others in ways that show they have worth and value and being considerate of other people's feelings. At Level 1, all youth baseball players should treat their coaches with respect. That does not change at Level 2. In fact, a **COMPLETE ATHLETE** always shows respect for his coaches at every level of play.

At Level 2, it's important for youth baseball players to learn to respect their teammates as well. The key is to treat them the way you would like them to treat you.

HOW TO DEMONSTRATE RESPECT FOR YOUR TEAMMATES AND OPPONENTS »

- Learn and address your teammates by their names.
- Listen carefully when a teammate is talking to you.
- Do not insult or talk about teammates and opponents behind their backs.
- When others make a mistake, forgive them and do not make fun of them.
- Let your teammates know you appreciate them both on and off the field.

SPORTSMANSHIP

Good **SPORTSMANSHIP** starts with respect for one's teammates, opponents, coaches, and officials. At Level 1, all youth baseball players should know the basic rules of baseball and always play by the rules. That does not change at Level 2. In fact, a **COMPLETE ATHLETE** always plays by the rules at every level of play.

At Level 2, youth baseball players begin to differentiate themselves by their skill levels. They begin to develop high expectations for themselves as well as their teammates. Often, it's the players that put in the most effort in terms of preparation who play the best.

However, some boys who practice regularly and try hard may not develop beyond a certain skill level. At Level 2, youth baseball players learn to accept players who have different levels of ability.

HOW TO TREAT TEAMMATES WITH LESS SKILL THAN YOU >>

- Never make fun of or insult a teammate.
- Do not talk about them behind their backs.
- Acknowledge any good plays they make.
- Reassure them if they make a poor play.
- Encourage them to improve by practicing skills with them outside of regular team practices.

ATHLETES >> There are many differences between a 12-year-old and a 14-year-old. Even kids that are the same age have different body types and different strengths. Some of them are more mature than others.

When I was this age, I played for a travel league team. Over two seasons, we won only a handful of games; yet, despite those losses, we had a good time, and I learned a great deal. We started to overachieve and win games we weren't expected to win, and that was a fun experience. But we also lost a lot of games. We learned a great deal about how to handle losing, which made me a much better player when I arrived in high school and, eventually, when I played pro ball. By playing on a team that was less talented than most of the competition, I worked much harder each play and every game so we could overcome our collective shortcomings or inexperience.

What I noticed was how much the older kids improved alongside the younger ones because they also learned to give extra effort and play harder. I learned from adversity, especially when it came to sportsmanship. It was interesting to watch how better teams handled losing to us; some handled it gracefully, and some threw fits. I also watched how the better teams reacted when they clobbered us.

Watching those blowout losses, I couldn't wait until the next time we played in the hopes that we would have grown and improved. Those kind of moments taught me the importance of good sportsmanship, whether you're losing or winning. Having those skills becomes even more pivotal when there's more pressure and the games grow more intense.

COACH MIKE MARTIN » *You've got to be able to control your emotions. Sportsmanship is all about controlling your emotions. There are times in our sport where you lose a game with two outs in the ninth inning. And you don't really want to go over there immediately and shake the guy's hand. But you look over at him, and if he is walking toward you, you walk to him—because that's what you should do as an athlete, as a leader. The winning coach should wait for the losing coach to initiate movement toward him.*

Players don't shake hands until the end of the series. But when players see coaches displaying sportsmanship every night, they learn how to conduct themselves and stay in control. Sometimes it's difficult, but it's important because sportsmanship is such a crucial part of athletics—and of developing men.

JOIN THE CONVERSATION!

For more coaching tips, be sure to check out the **COMPLETE ATHLETE** app.

TEAMWORK

TEAMWORK means working together as a group in order to achieve a goal. In sports, players contribute their individual skills and efforts in cooperation with their teammates to win games. Learning to play as part of a team—and not just as an individual athlete—is important at every level of play.

At Level 2, baseball coaches may add team-building exercises to practice sessions. Youth baseball players need to take these exercises seriously. Learning how to trust each other helps teammates work together more effectively and, ultimately, win more games.

COACHES » Travel ball teams at this level have long seasons. The best of these teams have learned how to bond well despite players coming from different cities. Most successful programs focus on team building early on, after tryouts are over but before tournaments begin.

It's important to build a team early, when players and parents are still excited and burnout hasn't kicked in. These kids and their families are going to be together for quite a while; it's worth the investment of a little extra time early on to get them to connect.

Find out who your parents and players are. Reach out to them when things are still new and exciting, before the team has blown a game or lost a tournament.

Everything and everyone is still overwhelmingly positive at this point. Hold pizza nights or barbecues to help everyone get to know one another.

The more the parents and the kids know everybody else, the better the chances of the team gelling. A lot of the best teams have players and parents bond quickly, and they often remain friends long after their sons' teams have moved on and baseball has ended.

PROFESSIONALISM

Certainly a youth athlete is not a professional in the sense of being paid to play. However, developing the attitude and behaviors of a **PROFESSIONAL** can help him more easily move up through the levels.

At Level 1, a youth baseball player learns to arrive on time with all his equipment at hand. However, it's likely that his parents have helped him by regularly washing his uniform and helping keep track of his equipment.

At Level 2, a youth baseball player should begin to take responsibility for keeping his equipment clean and well-maintained and for washing and folding his uniform properly. At this age, he should also take responsibility for his personal hygiene by showering regularly and always wearing deodorant so he can arrive at practices and games well-groomed and ready to go to work.

ATHLETES >> Hygiene, appearance, smell, and a neat uniform are all important in appearing professional and becoming a **COMPLETE ATHLETE**. When you see a pitcher on the mound with his shirt untucked or a position player with his pockets hanging out, he looks careless and sloppy.

We had a player who came in regularly whose equipment smelled awful because he never cleaned it. (Catchers' gear can get sweaty, and if it's not taken care of or kept in a closed bag, that equipment can smell like a locker room.) Even worse, the player looked terrible during his games, his back pockets always hanging out. He was also the one player who forgot his bat, gloves, and jackets all the time. We had to sit him down and gently explain to him that once he moved on to high school, coaches weren't going to take him seriously if he looked and acted as if he didn't take care of himself. They would assume he would not represent the program well.

Athletes need to take more responsibility at this level. Parents should not have to do everything anymore. Even middle school players are old enough to know to wear tucked-in shirts, clean pants, and the right uniform. This type of professionalism will pay off in the future.

COACHES >> Your appearance matters! Sometimes you may be rushing from work or one of your children's games, but it is very important that your appearance be appropriate for the game—especially if you want to set a good example for your players. I have attended games where the third-base coach had on shorts and a tank top while coaching his team. This shows you don't care enough to put time into looking professional.

Whenever possible, coaches should be wearing baseball pants and a jersey or a lightweight pullover with your team logo or name of a sponsor. Small things matter, and if you demonstrate that, the players will follow your example. How do you get upset with a player for forgetting to wear the right uniform or bring his belt if you have shown you don't care about these same details? Small things matter, and if you demonstrate that, the players will follow your example.

JOIN THE CONVERSATION!

Don't miss out on additional tips on teamwork, leadership, and professionalism from coaches and professionals in the **COMPLETE ATHLETE** app."

LEADERSHIP

A good leader is able to inspire and motivate others to do things they would not normally do or perform better than they would on their own. Developing leadership skills can benefit a youth athlete not only in high school and college but also in his professional life.

At Level 1, a youth baseball player begins to develop an understanding of what it takes to be an effective leader by watching how his coaches inspire and motivate him and his teammates. At Level 2, he can begin to display some of the leadership skills he has observed by looking out for and encouraging less-talented players on the team. For instance, he may invite a less-talented player to work with him outside of a regular practice session.

ATHLETES >> We had an eighth-grader who was one of the top pitchers in the state for his age. He was better than some of the high school pitchers two or three years older. While on a travel ball team, he became frustrated because the catcher he was working with was overmatched and letting a lot of balls pass. The pitcher asked us privately if we could have the catcher work with high school players and learn more.

The catcher struggled at first but quickly got better. Before he knew it, he was catching pitchers years older than himself and, eventually, pro pitchers, even though he hadn't yet caught one inning in high school. Even cooler, he later became a Division I catcher after two years in junior college.

The pitcher showed great leadership because he wanted to help the catcher grow as a player, but he didn't want to embarrass him or call him out. It was impressive to see this kid take on that role and try to make the players around him better.

BRENTON SULLIVAN >> *All organizations and all coaches have a type of player they like to recruit. This is definitely true for college, but it can be true for travel ball leagues too. Don't count yourself out just because you aren't as physically mature as other players. Some coaches will go after the biggest players, of course, but other coaches like to build their teams with talented players who feel overlooked and have something to prove. They often play much harder rather than taking their talent for granted. Great leaders, even at earlier levels, are players who respect the game and their team—not necessarily the star athletes of the league.*

2.2 PREPARATION

You will recall from Level 1 that **PREPARATION** refers to off-the-field activities, such as practicing skills, eating right, staying hydrated, getting enough rest, and mentally preparing for a game or practice. Coaches love athletes who prepare: these are the players who are eager to learn, eager to play, and ultimately, eager to win. They are the athletes that coaches want to help succeed because they already have a winning attitude. Preparation also helps athletes feel positive and confident in their ability to perform.

A **COMPLETE ATHLETE** prepares to perform on the field of play by continuously improving on the following:

PRACTICE

NUTRITION

HYDRATION

RECOVERY

MENTALITY

PRACTICE

At Level 1, a youth baseball player **PRACTICES** the basic techniques of baseball with an emphasis on having fun and becoming a better, more confident player. At Level 2, a youth baseball player continues to work on mastering the basic techniques through individual practice sessions. He also begins to work on becoming a well-rounded player by understanding—and practicing—all positions involved in the game of baseball. Learning all positions also helps the youth baseball player begin to narrow down his choices for specialization at higher levels of play.

As in Level 1, the more focused a youth athlete remains during his individual practice sessions, the more effective the practice time will be. The idea is to work smarter—not harder or longer. Creating a practice schedule with specific drills to practice can help a youth baseball player better focus during these sessions.

LEVEL 2 SAMPLE PRACTICE SESSION >>

• Warm up and stretch
• Drill 1 — based on position skills
• Drill 2 — based on position skills
• Drill 3 — based on position skills

PRIVATE COACHING >>

Starting at Level 2, a youth baseball player who is serious about moving into higher levels of play and possibly earning a college scholarship should consider working with a private coach. Working on basic techniques with a private coach can give a youth baseball player a huge advantage over other players his age.

Most private coaches provide one-on-one sessions that are focused on the individual player and customized based on the skills he most needs to improve. They generally work on hitting, pitching, catching, agility, speed, tactical understanding, and decision making to help a baseball player reach his maximum potential.

PARENTS >> This is an important time for baseball players to ask with whom they should be working. Coaches have a limited amount of time for travel ball or Little League teams. Finding a specialized instructor for private lessons is important and can play a huge role in improving the player.

When youth travel baseball tryouts are near, I tell kids things are about to change dramatically. Teams have cuts. Just because you sign up for tryouts, doesn't mean you will be placed on a team. Little League teams draw from the same city. With such a small pool, the kids all know who the better players are. Once they start travel ball, they are trying out for teams with players from different cities. Most of these kids are constantly working hard to improve, which means players have to step up their game at this level. Those who don't improve will probably fall behind the kids who are either getting private lessons or practicing more on their own. Not all kids need to have private lessons, but I encourage them for anyone who can.

I had a scheduled evaluation with a player, the first time I had seen him up close. He clearly needed some work, especially on arm strength. I asked what his goal was, and he said he was getting ready for a big tryout with a travel ball team. I knew that travel ball team, and this kid wasn't ready for it. While he had been a Little League All-Star, he had not played in a year and wasn't aware that the travel ball team brought in kids from other cities. He had barely thrown or practiced since playing in Little League. He and his parents simply didn't do their homework. Because he hadn't been working on his skills, he was not in a good position to succeed. Even worse, with such little preparation, he could have been seriously injured. He should have begun private lessons far earlier.

NUTRITION

NUTRITION plays a key role in athletic performance. Youth athletes are building muscle, burning calories, and growing. They need to eat and drink regularly to make up for calories they are burning and fluids they are using during practice and actual games.

An active youth baseball player needs to consume healthy food and beverages to aid with the following:

- Replenishing his energy supply
- Maintaining hydration
- Obtaining the vitamins and minerals needed to support metabolism, tissue growth, and repair
- Preventing injuries and/or illnesses
- Performing at his best both on and off the field

GENERAL SPORTS NUTRITION GUIDELINES »

- All athletes should consume five or more balanced meals spread throughout the day, every 3 to 4 hours.
- Meals should be eaten 2 to 3 hours before practice or games, and snacks eaten 1 to 1.5 hours hours before practice or games.
- Eat when you're hungry to prevent lean-muscle breakdown; stop when you're full to prevent being sluggish.
- Eat breakfast within 30 minutes of waking to prevent lean-muscle breakdown, increase energy and concentration, and maintain good blood-sugar control. Choose whole grains, fresh fruit, and lean protein for breakfast.
- Eat well-balanced meals and snacks consisting of carbohydrates, lean proteins, and heart-healthy fats.

- Drink a protein shake or eat a snack or meal that has equal amounts protein and carbohydrates within 30 minutes of a workout.
- Choose fresh, whole foods whenever possible (instead of processed foods that are packaged or refined) to increase nutritional value. Avoid foods that are high in sugar and/or trans fat.

LEVEL-2 ATHLETE NUTRITION GUIDELINES »

Each individual has different macronutrient needs, based on height, weight, age, activity level, and genetic background. The following macronutrient guidelines are based on age and estimated activity level for a Level 2 athlete:

- 55 percent carbohydrate
- 20 percent protein
- 25 percent fat
- No more than 7 percent saturated fat
- No trans fat
- 31 grams of fiber per day
- No more than 150 calories per day from sugar (37.5 grams or 9 teaspoons)

Just as in Level 1, a Level 2 youth baseball player should choose from the following to fulfill the macronutrient needs listed above:

CARBOHYDRATES High-fiber foods, such as whole-grain bread, brown rice, whole-grain pasta (or gluten-free versions), beans, starchy vegetables (e.g., corn, peas, potatoes), quinoa, and cereal.

PROTEINS Chicken, turkey, or fish, especially wild salmon, tuna, trout, mackerel, and sardines, which are all high in heart-healthy omega-3 fatty acids.

FATS Low-fat cheese, nuts/nut butters (natural peanut butter or almond butter), avocados, seeds, and heart-healthy oils such as extra-virgin olive oil, canola oil, grapeseed oil, and flaxseed oil

VEGETABLES Preferably leafy green vegetables

ATHLETES » At this level, nutrition becomes more of a factor. Some kids with really good genes can eat whatever they want and stay lean and strong. Other kids aren't blessed with those kinds of genes. We had an eighth-grader who had been working out with us for a while. He showed up regularly and worked pretty hard. This made him stronger. He hit the ball harder and threw better. But he was still out of shape and had too much body fat. He was missing the most important element of getting stronger and in shape—his diet.

Think of your workouts as the exposed part of an iceberg and your diet as the much larger part hidden under the surface. Just like that part of the iceberg, your diet is larger and often overlooked.

Over the summer, this player redirected himself and focused on nutrition while continuing to be a beast in the gym. He only lost about 5 pounds, but he gained lots of muscle. He had more energy and better workouts. When we asked him what he had changed, he said he cut out soda, drank water, and eliminated fast food. This helped him improve so much that he became the best player on his high school team.

HYDRATION

All athletes need to drink water before, during, and after practices and games. This is especially important on days when both temperatures and humidity levels are high. If a youth baseball player does not drink enough water, he could suffer from dehydration.

HOW TO MAINTAIN PROPER HYDRATION* >>

- Before exercise, drink 16 to 20 full ounces within the two-hour period prior to exercise.
- During exercise, drink 4 to 6 full ounces.
- After exercise, replace 24 full ounces for every one pound of body weight lost during exercise.

ATHLETES >> Drinking water sounds simple, but it's important and could have implications beyond cramps. We had an eighth-grader, a very skilled player, who was out on the East Coast for the first time at a big tournament. This pitcher was ranked very high in his age group based on his performance in previous tournaments. USA Baseball representatives were going to be on hand to watch him pitch and consider inviting him to their tryouts at their headquarters in Cary, North Carolina.

This athlete was used to California's dry heat and was not ready for the high humidity, which impacted his pitching. Back home, he pitched in the mid-80s, which is impressive for someone his age. But things were different here, and his velocity dropped to 77–78 mph due to the humidity.

Adapted from guidelines provided by the American College of Sports Medicine (ACSM)

He felt sick and dizzy because he did not have enough water in him. He perspired so much that his entire jersey was soaked, and the heat drained his energy.

USA Baseball told his coach after the game that his velocity wasn't where it needed to be. While they promised to do their best to see him again, that didn't happen until a year later. The kid was embarrassed, but if he had prepared for the humidity and drank a little more water, things would have been different.

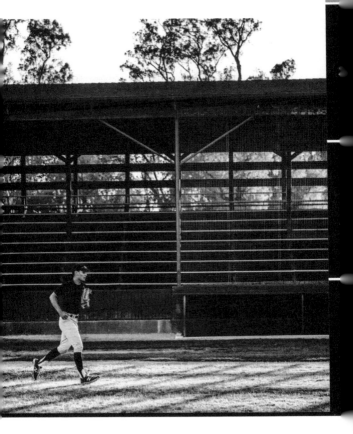

RECOVERY

Youth baseball players need to eat and drink within 30 minutes of a practice or game to make up for calories they are burning and fluids they are using. Replenishing calories and fluids also aids in muscle recovery and repair.

HOW TO REPLENISH CALORIES AND FLUIDS »

- Drink 24 ounces of fluid for every pound of sweat lost within two hours of a game or practice.
- Consume 15 grams of protein plus an equal amount of carbohydrates within the 30-minute recovery window.

SLEEP »

Just as increased activity creates a greater need for calories, it also creates a greater need for sleep. An athlete's body does its growing, healing, and muscle repair during sleep. Recovery also refers to allowing the body to rest and heal from the demands of practices and games.

According to the National Sleep Foundation, a Level 2 youth athlete should get 10 to 11 hours of sleep each night for proper growth and development. If that's not possible, or if he needs additional recovery time, he should look at his weekly schedule and plan how he can incorporate extra sleep or rest time. To get the additional rest he needs, he can take short naps (no more than 30 minutes) or engage in quiet rest periods (lying down, reading, or watching TV).

ATHLETES » Sleep plays an important role for any travel ball team. In seventh grade, I took part in my first out-of-state travel ball tournament.

Like many summer tournaments, this one was going to be in a different time zone. Thus, our coach told us to go to bed an hour earlier two weeks before the tournament, and go to sleep an hour earlier and wake an hour earlier the week before the tournament. Two days before we left, our coach made sure we went to sleep on East Coast time. Because he planned this ahead of time, it was no trouble to follow.

Unfortunately, not everyone did. On the first night, the parents all went out to dinner. While they were out, we had a good time, running around, burning energy, and tiring ourselves out. Some stayed up too late and paid the price the next morning. Even worse, we played a well-rested team from the East Coast, and they beat us. Our coach was upset and said it was obvious who was fresh and ready to play and who was not. That loss put us in the losers bracket, and we were knocked out in the quarterfinals.

MENTALITY

At Level 2, a baseball player can step up his mental practice. Certainly, a youth baseball player should step up and spend more time physically preparing his body to meet the demands of a practice session or game. Similarly, engaging in mental preparation can help a young athlete perform at a higher level by creating the proper mindset for either a practice or game.

At Level 1, a youth baseball player mentally prepares by closing his eyes, breathing deeply, and envisioning himself having fun on the baseball field. This is also a great activity to practice at Level 2.

In addition, a youth baseball player should engage in activities that help him build confidence in his abilities and push him to higher levels of performance.

HOW TO BUILD CONFIDENCE >>

- Reflect on all the positive feedback you've gotten from your coaches.
- Tell yourself that you're a great player, you worked hard this week and are a solid member of the team.
- Think about the constructive feedback you've received and remind yourself that those people want to see you succeed.
- Disregard any negative comments (even if they're from your parents) and focus only on positive comments.
- Don't beat yourself up when you make a mistake; instead, focus on doing better next time.
- Continue to practice on your own. When you complete a successful practice session, your confidence rises.
- The more you practice, the higher your confidence will become.

COACHES >> Players at this level can start practicing visualization exercises. For example, they can pick spots on a field or at a stadium to help relax and focus during a game. I tell kids to pick a stationary object before the game and focus on it when they need to relax and clear their minds. This is a good habit that can stick with a player for a long time. I once went to watch a high-level player pitch. The week before, we had talked about picking a focal point during the game. Before the first pitch, he stepped off the mound and looked out toward left field where there was an old tree. The tree was almost dead, which made it stand out since the trees around it were green. I knew he had made that tree his focal point. He pitched a very good game. At our next session, we talked about that game, and he said the old tree had been his focal point. He said focusing on the tree allowed him to slow down and remember some of the things he had been working on. Focusing allowed him to take a breath, slow down the game, and concentrate on the right things. By having that focal point, he had more confidence to go out and pitch.

DANIEL ROBERTSON » *Recovering from an ACL tear in junior high was tough, but my mentality helped get me through it. Because I was so young, the doctor wanted to wait for a growth spurt before he drilled into my knee. He actually told me I would not be playing baseball for two years, until I was 16. I didn't accept that. I remember thinking how much I loved playing baseball and I knew nothing was going to take it away from me.*

I knew how hard I worked determined how quickly I would be able to play. I was in rehab for four months and did not pick up a ball or a bat during that time. I went to rehab every day and did all I could to improve each time. It made me value how hard I worked and how much time I spent practicing and becoming a better baseball player. All the rehab paid off as I returned to the field. I had to play with a knee brace for two years before the surgery was performed, but I refused to accept spending those two years away from the game I loved so much.

JOIN THE CONVERSATION!

Step up your mental game with more tips in the **COMPLETE ATHLETE** app.

FITNESS

FITNESS matters. A baseball player needs to develop strength and speed to play the game effectively and prevent injuries. He also needs a high degree of mobility. Mobility is the ability to move through a full range of motion. A **COMPLETE ATHLETE** maintains a high degree of the following:

LOWER-BODY STRENGTH

UPPER-BODY STRENGTH

FLEXIBILITY / MOBILITY

CORE STRENGTH

SPEED / QUICKNESS / ENDURANCE

In Level 1, a number of exercises were discussed to improve a youth baseball player's overall fitness. At Level 2, a youth baseball player should be able to perform all Level 1 tests at a higher degree in terms of time and distance. These exercises are revisited below and several more are introduced.

BRENTON SULLIVAN >> *Every coach is looking for future potential. At this level, players mature at different rates. Some athletes become frustrated and may feel tempted to give up before their body has had a chance to grow and change. Just because other players may be maturing faster than you, don't think that you are always going to be behind.*

Even if you are not the biggest guy on the team entering high school, don't think that means college coaches aren't going to look at you. They have a good eye for spotting potential. They can often look at a player and know, "This guy may be wiry now, but with real weight training, he can really fill out his frame." In other words, don't quit just because you're small right now. That won't last forever.

LOWER-BODY STRENGTH

LOWER-BODY STRENGTH is becoming more important than it was in Level 1. You are becoming more advanced and should be learning how to use your legs in your swings and throws. By putting more work into your lower-body strength, you will begin to see significant speed gains, quicker cutting, better footwork, and greater power in your hitting and throwing. If the lower-body is neglected, a baseball player can fatigue quickly and risk injuries when he starts to push his body harder in more competitive environments such as travel ball and tournaments.

The lateral jump will be added to your Level 2 testing. It will test your side-to-side leg power. It is important to have exceptional lateral movement in baseball, as it allows pitchers to stride farther with more power and fielders to cover more ground. The single-leg test is still very important to show if one leg is dominant. A well-balanced athlete is a healthy athlete.

TO PERFORM SINGLE-LEG WALL SIT

• Stand with your back against a smooth wall, feet approximately shoulder-width apart.
• Slowly slide your back down the wall until both knees and hips are at a 90-degree angle.
• Lift one foot of the ground and hold it as long as possible. After a period of rest, lift the other foot and hold it.

NOTE >> If you can hold one foot up considerably longer than the other, you may need to work on developing a better balance of strength in both legs.

TO PERFORM A BROAD JUMP >>

- Stand behind a line marked on the ground, feet slightly apart.
- Use a two-foot takeoff and landing, swinging the arms and bending the knees to provide forward drive.
- Jump as far as possible, landing on both feet without falling backward.

TO PERFORM A LATERAL JUMP >>

- Stand on one leg with the foot at the starting line and hands on hips.
- Squat down quickly and then jump sideways as far as possible, landing on both feet without losing balance.
- Measure the distance jumped to the nearest foot.

UPPER-BODY STRENGTH

In Level 1, **UPPER-BODY STRENGTH** was identified as an important but overlooked aspect of baseball fitness. Now, upper-body strength starts to play a major role in athleticism and, most importantly, your arm health. A strong upper-body also helps protect the arm in deceleration from throwing at high intensities. Fields are bigger than at Level 1, and the ability to hit and throw greater distances with more power can be the difference in making desired teams.

When a player throws a baseball, the throwing arm both accelerates and decelerates. The decelerator muscle groups are like the car brakes; they allow the fast-moving body parts to slow down. In baseball, strong back muscles are important for safe deceleration during throwing actions. The better your brakes, the more velocity can be gained without risking your health. This is especially important for pitchers, who throw the ball more often than any other position player.

As discussed in Level 1, pull exercises such as the flexed-arm hang are used to increase upper back strength and mobility, while push exercises such as push-ups increase chest and shoulder strength and mobility.

TO PERFORM A FLEXED-ARM HANG >>

- Grasp an overhead bar using an underhand grip (palms facing toward body).
- Position the body with arms flexed and the chin clearing the bar. The chest should be held close to the bar, legs hanging straight.
- Hold this position as long as possible.

TO PERFORM PUSH-UPS »

- Lie facedown on the floor (or mat) with hands under the shoulders or slightly wider than the chest, fingers straight, legs straight and parallel.
- Straighten the arms, pushing the upper-body up and keeping the back and knees straight.
- Bend the arms to lower the upper-body until the elbows are at a 90-degree angle and the upper arms are parallel to the floor.
- Perform as many repetitions as possible without resting.

ROTATIONAL MEDICINE BALL THROWS follow the same motor pattern used in games. They help to teach youth baseball players how to transfer power from rotational movements such as swinging and throwing. It may be the single most important component in training to hit and throw harder.

TO PERFORM A ROTATIONAL MEDICINE BALL THROW

- Stand perpendicular to a start line (such as in a pitching or hitting stance).
- Hold a medicine ball in both hands, placing back hand on the back of the ball and the front hand under the ball.
- Draw the ball back with only a slight bend at the elbows, keeping the ball between the waist and chest.
- In one swift motion, fling the ball up and forward (optimally at a 45-degree angle).

JOIN THE CONVERSATION!

Fitness is essential to becoming a **COMPLETE ATHLETE**. Learn more by downloading the app and checking out the *tips & techniques* videos!

FLEXIBILITY / MOBILITY

A good degree of **FLEXIBILITY** and **MOBILITY** leads to better baseball technique and helps to prevent injuries. As discussed in Level 1, the sit-and-reach test is used to assess and improve a youth athlete's level of lower-body flexibility and mobility. Likewise, the shoulder-stretch test is used to assess and improve a youth athlete's level of upper-body flexibility and mobility.

TO PERFORM THE SIT-AND-REACH TEST »

NOTE » You'll need a box that is 12 inches high, such as a milk crate. Tape a yardstick or ruler to the top so that the first 9 inches hang over the edge and the 9-inch mark is exactly on the edge against which you will place your feet.

- Place the box against a wall.
- Sit on the floor in front of the box with your legs straight in front of you and the soles of your feet flat against the front side of the box. (The overhanging part of the ruler should be pointed at your chest or midsection.)
- Keeping the legs straight and flat on the floor, stretch forward and reach along the ruler with one hand on top of the other, palms down.
- Stretch forward three times without bouncing; then reach as far as possible, holding at the farthest point for at least three seconds.

TO PERFORM THE SHOULDER-STRETCH TEST »

- Stand with feet slightly apart.
- Place one hand behind the head and back over the shoulder with the palm touching your body and fingers directed downward.

- Place the other arm behind your back, palm facing outward and fingers upward.
- Reach as far as possible, attempting to touch the fingers of each hand together.
- Repeat with the other side.

CORE STRENGTH

CORE STRENGTH at Level 2 should be a high priority in your daily training regimen. Just as they do with nutrition, some athletes overlook keeping up their core exercises. If this is the case, you will be more likely to have a back injury or even one of those pesky oblique injuries that tend to nag athletes and keep them off the field. A strong core is the glue for all the strength you are putting into your lower- and upper-body.

Testing will point out any neglect to your core strength and let you know where you should improve to protect your health.

As in Level 1, we have included a plank and medicine ball throw, but we have added the hip-lift march to test lower back, gluteal, and hamstring strength.

TO PERFORM A PLANK >>

- Get down on the floor with your hands apart slightly wider than shoulder-width, your arms straight and supporting your weight.
- Make sure your body stays straight. Your hips shouldn't be sticking way up in the air or sagging.
- Hold that position as long as you can.

TO PERFORM A SIDE PLANK »

• Lie on your side with your legs straight.
• Prop up your upper-body on your elbow and forearm.
• Make sure your elbow is aligned with the shoulder.
• Brace your core by contracting your abs forcefully,
  and then raise your hips until your body forms a
  straight line from your ankles to your shoulders.
• Breathe deeply while holding this position.
• Repeat this exercise on your other side.

The **HIP-LIFT MARCH** helps to measure (and improve)
the strength and endurance of the lower back muscles.

TO PERFORM A HIP-LIFT MARCH »

• Lie flat on your back, knees bent 90 degrees and feet
  flat on the ground.
• Lift hips as high as possible; only shoulders and feet
  should touch the ground.
• Keeping hips at the same height, lift each knee in a
  controlled marching motion for as long as possible.

SPEED / QUICKNESS / ENDURANCE

As discussed in Level 1, there are two types of
baseball speed:

• Straightaway speed on the base paths or in the outfield
• Lateral (side-to-side) quickness, such as when an
  infielder moves to get a ground ball.

The 30-yard sprint helps an athlete improve straight-away speed. The 5-10-5 Shuttle Run, or Pro Agility Drill, is a great way to improve lateral **QUICKNESS** because it helps to hone an athlete's ability to accelerate, decelerate, stop, and reaccelerate without losing balance. The Beep Test is a good way to measure and improve endurance.

TO PERFORM A 5-10-5 SHUTTLE RUN »

- Set up three marker cones 5 yards apart.
- Start at the middle marker cone in a three-point stance.
- Turn and run 5 yards to the right side and touch the marker cone with the right hand.
- Turn around and run 10 yards to the left and touch the marker cone with the left hand.
- Finish by running back to the middle marker cone.

TO PERFORM A BEEP TEST »

NOTE » You'll first need to download a Beep Test audio recording or Beep Test app, which will play beeps at set intervals. As the test proceeds, the interval between each successive beep reduces, forcing the athlete to increase his speed.

- Draw two lines 20 yards apart.
- Stand behind one of the lines, face the second line, and begin running when instructed by the recording.
- Continue running between the two lines, turning when signaled by the recorded beeps. After about one minute, a sound indicates an increase in speed, and the beeps will be closer together.
- The test is stopped when the athlete can no longer keep in sync with the recording.

LEVEL-2 FITNESS TEST

LOWER-BODY STRENGTH
- Single-leg wall sit of 40 seconds on each leg
- Broad jump of 85 inches
- Lateral jump of 75 inches or greater

UPPER-BODY STRENGTH
- Flexed-arm hang of 20 seconds
- 25 push-ups in 60 seconds
- Rotational medicine ball throw of at least 30 feet with an 8-pound. ball

FLEXIBILITY/MOBILITY
- At least 32 centimeters in the sit-and-reach test
- Shoulder-stretch test (pass or fail)

CORE STRENGTH
- 2.5-minute plank
- 30-second side plank on each side
- Hip-lift march with perfect form for 90 seconds
- Balance 30 seconds on each leg

SPEED/QUICKNESS/ENDURANCE
- 5-10-5 Shuttle Run in 5.3 seconds
- 30-yard sprint in 4.5 seconds
- Beep Test minimum score of Level 7

JOIN THE CONVERSATION!

For more fitness tips and how-to's, download the **COMPLETE ATHLETE** app now!

2.4 TECHNIQUE

In just about any sport, basic **TECHNIQUES** are the most important skills to master. These skills are the building blocks upon which more advanced skills are learned. At Level 2, a youth baseball player needs to build on the basic skills covered in Level 1:

THROWING

HITTING

INFIELD FIELDING

OUTFIELD FIELDING

GAME ASSESSMENT

Building on these skills involves displaying the same proper mechanics while moving faster and with more accuracy. As a youth athlete moves up, throwing strength becomes more important. Throwing strength is measured by the distance and speed with which a player is able to throw the ball. Level 2 also requires an understanding of situational hitting and pitching.

JON OLSEN >> *Study athletes you respect, ones with similar mechanics and playing styles to yours. For me, I really like to analyze how Adam Wainwright performs in every game. He's someone who improves as the game goes on and is better in the ninth inning than he was in the first. Rather than tiring or wearing down, he ramps up his game as he goes. I also respect his demeanor because he is always consistent.*

That's the kind of player I want to be, so I watch him carefully to see if I can pick up mechanical cues from him—any little thing that might help me get ahead. Be yourself as a player, but also study the guys you want to be like and see what you can learn from how they play the game.

THROWING

High-quality **THROWING** technique requires accuracy, arm strength, and proper mechanics to make plays. As you are required to throw greater distances, you will need to increase your effort without losing the integrity of your mechanics. This can be done easily if you focus on slowly building your arm strength with long-toss and shoulder exercise programs. At Level 2, technique does not change, but a player must maintain accuracy as distance increases.

NOTE >> At the beginning of Appendix 1, you will find a "Return to Throwing" breakdown that I put together with Alan Jaeger of Jaeger Sports. It will guide you through a routine to give your arm the rest it needs and the plan to then get it back into game shape. I recommend taking 2 to 3 months off from competitive throwing every 12 months. They can be broken into two periods of 4 to 6 weeks.

TECHNICAL TIPS >>

When throwing a ball, keep these goals in mind:

• Keep your body under control and eyes on the target.
• Use shuffle throws for distances of 75 to 90 feet.
• Use crow-hop throws for distances greater than 90 feet.
• When throwing greater distances, keep your weight back and your front shoulder slightly higher than your back shoulder.
• As you complete the throw, finish in a balanced, controlled position.

COMMON MISTAKES >>

• Rushing your throws
• Throwing off balance
• Long arm paths
• Inconsistent landings after ball release
• Overthrowing
• Rushing footwork
• Forgetting to focus on hitting a small target

DIFFERENT POSITIONS REQUIRE DIFFERENT SKILLS

Infielders need to make five consecutive, accurate throws from the shortstop position:

• With shuffle
• Using a backhand position one step
• From a running position

Outfielders need to make five consecutive, accurate throws from right field to second base and two consecutive, accurate throws from right field to home, all within a 6-foot radius.

A catcher's pop time to second base should be less than 2.35 seconds, and he should be able to hit his target a minimum of three out of five times.

A pitcher needs to throw accurately from the bullpen with a 65 percent strike ratio or greater:

• 30 fastball pitches
• 15 from stretch position
• 15 from windup

HITTING

HITTING should be practiced more than any other skill in baseball. Merely making contact isn't going to be enough now. You must learn to drive the ball and know what approach to take in certain situations. You should also be familiar with your swing by now and probably have had some private coaching or self-teaching to identify your flaws. You should know how to hit a line drive on hanging pitches and should now work on bunting, moving runners, and pitch selection. Use batting practice for more than hitting home runs. Practice moving runners, lifting the ball, keeping the ball on the ground, and swinging at strikes.

In Level 1, basic hitting technique was discussed. It is summarized below:

When attempting to hit the ball, swing aggressively once you see your pitch. Stay relaxed and take deep breaths between pitches.

At Level 2, baseball fields are larger with greater distances. This can result in slower pitching than what was experienced at Level 1. Therefore, a youth baseball player must stay back and be a little more patient. Try not to jump out to swing at slow pitches.

TECHNICAL TIPS >>

- Stay quiet in your lower half.
- Practice hitting the ball to opposite fields and center field.
- Recognize breaking balls. During practice, have a coach mix them in or use a batting machine that can throw breaking balls.
- Always be ready to hit a fastball and adjust to off-speed pitches.

INFIELD FIELDING

INFIELD FIELDING refers to catching balls in the infield. Level 2 infielders are becoming strong at routine plays and able to make plays and throws in the hole. If you are in the middle infield, you need to put added focus on the exchange from glove to hand to throw.

Third basemen should be working on keeping everything in front of them and fielding bunts or slow-hit balls. First basemen need to work on catching short hops from throws across the diamond along with turning double plays to second and home. Infielders should be able to catch both ground balls and pop flies with either their backhand or forehand and while moving. At this level, balls will be hit with greater velocity and cover more ground. Fielding must be clean.

TO REVIEW >>

To properly catch a ground ball, bend your knees, balance on the balls of your feet, and get your glove down on the ground with your bare hand close by. If a slow ground ball comes to you, run toward it to cut time and distance.

To properly catch a pop fly, keep an eye on the ball as it moves through the air. Get under the ball and catch it with two hands, one hand in the glove and one covering the glove after you make the catch.

If trying to catch a ball on the run, you can use only your glove to make the catch. Always run to where you think the ball will land and prepare for the catch.

TECHNICAL TIPS >>

- Make sure the glove is in contact with the ground when attempting to make a play.
- Catch the ball cleanly, ready to make an athletic move.
- Use your knees, not your waist, to lower yourself to the ground.
- Get your body into position to keep ball in front of you.

COMMON MISTAKES »

- Being afraid of the ball
- Not having the glove in good fielding position
- Not being ready or being flat-footed
- Arriving late to your fielding position
- Panicking if ball is bobbled

DIFFERENT POSITIONS REQUIRE DIFFERENT SKILLS

PITCHERS »

- Do not overthrow to reach the catcher at the new distance.
- Keep pitch counts low, building up your arm at new distance.
- Develop smart pitch selection.
- Learn to control the running game.
- Control your emotions while on the mound.

JON OLSEN » *As a pitcher, you have to learn to block out your emotions, something I've learned from another sport. Many people are surprised to hear it, but playing golf has helped my baseball career. I started playing golf when I was 3, and there are a lot of relatable concepts between the sports.*

Both of them are mental games where it's easy to get frustrated. Playing golf has helped me keep my cool over the years, even when I'm giving up a lot of hits in front of thousands of people. If you're too emotional out there, opposing teams will pick up on it and use it to their advantage. Playing baseball and golf has helped me learn to hide my emotions.

CATCHERS »

- Do not take balls out of the strike zone.
- Block three out of five balls in the dirt, within a 2-foot radius of your knees.
- Stay on your toes and be ready to move with runners on base.
- Control the running game by calling smart pitches and learning to block balls.

OUTFIELD FIELDING

The main activity in **OUTFIELD FIELDING** is catching fly balls and throwing them to the infield. Make sure you communicate with other outfielders and infielders, know how many outs there are, and know how to back up bases. An outfielder must be able to catch while running to the left, to the right, backward, and forward. He must also be able to throw the ball quickly and accurately. Outfielders must also be good at catching grounders, especially knowing when to scoop and go or break down and block a ball.

TO PROPERLY CATCH BALLS IN THE OUTFIELD »

- Stay calm and relaxed, but anticipate the ball before it is hit.
- Keep your glove in front of your face and above eye level when the ball is in the air and you are in position to make the catch.
- Keep an eye on the ball as it moves through the air and never run with your glove extended.
- Make sure your glove is down when fielding grounders.

Because fields are larger at Level 2, outfielders must be able to do the following:

- Catch balls on the run
- Cover more distance
- Have quicker reaction times with faster exchanges
- Maintain a high degree of accuracy—hit cutoffs!

GAME ASSESSMENT

GAME ASSESSMENT refers to the ability to perform the above techniques during an actual game, not just in practice. It also includes developing good judgment regarding in-game decisions. Game assessment is summarized below:

- Making accurate throws
- Fielding your position properly
- Making good contact off live pitches
- Making smart base-running decisions
- When pitching, throwing strikes at least 65 percent of the time
- Backing up other outfielders and bases
- Anticipating where the ball may be hit by knowing what pitch is being thrown (and what the hitter may do with it)
- Hitting your cutoff man 100 percent of the time

Different positions require different game assessment skills to make good on-field decisions, both defensively and offensively:

- Hitters should have quality at-bats.
- Pitchers should be throwing 65 percent strikes and
- controlling base runners. Pitches should take 1.4 seconds to the plate. They must be able to throw strikes at a 65 percent ratio in windup and stretch during a bullpen session.
- Catchers should be able to block balls with efficiency, improve pop times, and make accurate throws to bases.

To pass Level 2 Game Assessment, a youth athlete must have a coach assess him in the following:

- Accuracy
- Proper fielding
- Making smart base-running decisions
- Backing up other outfielders and bases
- Remaining fully focused before every pitch
- Understanding different pitching strategies (and what the hitter may do based on the pitch thrown)

JOIN THE CONVERSATION!

Download the **COMPLETE ATHLETE** app today! Available for iPhone and Android.

LEVEL-2 SKILLS TEST

THROWING »

- Display proper form, staying in control with eyes on
  your target and a well-balanced follow-through.
- Throw the baseball accurately five times from a
  distance of at least 150 feet within a 6-foot radius of
  the target.

HITTING »

- Perform situational hitting during front-toss practice
  with near-perfect reps off the tee and soft toss front toss.
- Hit line drives off the tee to all fields (left/center/right)
  five times in a row.
- Hit the ball five times in a row to all fields from a soft toss.

NOTE » The coach should toss balls in a way that will
make the batter hit the ball where it is pitched:

- Balls thrown to the inside should be pulled.
- Balls thrown outside should be hit opposite field.
- Balls down the middle should be hit to center field.

- Make hard contact off an overhand toss five times in a
  row. If the ball pops up or is missed at all, start over.

INFIELD FIELDING »

- Catch 10 ground balls consecutively, cleanly hit
  from a coach.

NOTE » Alternating from forehand to backhand while
running forward and straight at them. The athlete should

get four seconds to reset after making the catch. Make five quick, clean exchanges with accurate throws to target (e.g., shortstop to second base).

• Perform a range test, covering 10 yards in 1.2 seconds.

OUTFIELD FIELDING >>

• Catch fly balls thrown from the coach 10 times consecutively.

NOTE >> Set up a 15-yard radius circle in the outfield with the player standing in the center in a ready position. Coach will throw one ball at a time to alternating areas of the circle. Once the ball is caught, the player has 8 seconds to reset.

• Catch a ball hit to you off the bat five times in a row.

NOTE >> Balls should be hit at a height that requires the outfielder to move and catch balls on the run or set up properly and catch a fly ball.

• Catch the ball five times in a row on the run, thrown from the coach.

NOTE >> These balls should be similar to line drives. Catches should be made while running in both directions without losing stride: three balls to your left/back, three to your right/back, one running forward, and one straight back over your shoulder.

• Cleanly field five balls grounders and exchange the balls out of glove using proper throwing technique.

GAME ASSESSMENT >>

To pass Level 2 Game Assessment, a youth athlete must have a coach assess him in the following:

• Accuracy
• Proper fielding
• Making smart base-running decisions
• Backing up other outfielders and bases
• Remaining fully focused before every pitch
• Understanding different pitching strategies (and what the hitter may do based on the pitch thrown)

2.5 LIFESTYLE

As youth baseball players achieve higher levels of success, they will find the demands on their time increasing. Creating a healthy balance between sports, academics, family obligations, and social activities requires strong time-management skills and a clear understanding of what's important.

JOIN THE CONVERSATION!

Organization, academics, and your social life are all very important components to becoming a successful **COMPLETE ATHLETE**.
Learn more by downloading the app today!

As a youth baseball player moves into Level 2 during the middle school years, he should begin to develop strong organizational skills. Strong organizational skills can help him in all other areas of his life:

FAMILY

ACADEMICS

SOCIAL LIFE

ROLE MODEL

LIVING YOUR SPORT

FAMILY

As was discussed in Level 1, parents take on a fair amount of responsibility when their sons begin to play baseball. Parents are responsible for getting them to practices and games, both on their own and by forming carpools with other families. They help their sons obtain and pay for equipment, uniforms and more. And they often take time out of their busy schedules to attend games and cheer on their sons.

Youth baseball players who develop strong organizational skills tend to have stronger, more positive family relationships. For example, youth baseball players who keep track of practice and game schedules will know when their uniforms need to be clean and won't be asking mom or dad to wash their uniforms at the last minute. Youth baseball players who keep their equipment organized and in a safe place will always know right where to find everything they need for practice or a game. Also, being aware of any regularly scheduled activities of other family members helps a youth baseball player know when his parents are available for carpooling to special practices or other events.

ACADEMICS

In addition to maintaining good grades and behaving appropriately in class, which was discussed in Level 1, a youth baseball player must remember that school is more important than sports. In fact, if a coach's decision comes down to two athletes with the same amount of athleticism, the coach will almost always choose the athlete with the better grades. Higher **ACADEMIC** achievement also leads to more college acceptances and scholarship offers.

Middle school is obviously tougher than elementary school; nonetheless, grades must be maintained. Staying organized can go a long way toward helping a youth baseball player balance school and sports.

HOW TO STAY ORGANIZED >>

• Prioritize schoolwork and make to-do lists for getting it done.
• Do what works best for your personal working style. For instance, are you good at multitasking? Or do you work best by focusing on finishing one project at a time?

NOTE >> Some youth baseball players consider choosing a different high school from their zoned school so they can play for a certain coach. It's far better to make sure that the high school provides a solid academic program, which will help them better prepare for the SATs and get into the college of their choice.

SOCIAL LIFE

While many youth baseball players' social lives revolve around their teammates, many have friends outside of sports. Either way, a youth baseball player should develop a lifestyle that includes spending time with friends outside of the baseball and offline.

As was discussed in Level 1, a solid **SOCIAL LIFE** is important for all young people, not just youth athletes. Friends provide companionship and recreation. Friends also give advice to one another and often help ease anxiety during times of stress. Young people who don't have friends tend to be more lonely and unhappy, struggle academically, and have lower self-esteem.

Online socializing has become the norm for many young people. However, it's important for them to remember that their online life isn't a substitute for spending time with friends in person. Face-to-face socializing provides more of the benefits of friendship and helps youth athletes develop the interpersonal skills that are essential for success in all areas of life.

HOW TO FIND A HEALTHY BALANCE BETWEEN ONLINE AND IN-PERSON SOCIAL INTERACTIONS >>

If you think you type more than you speak to your friends, you may need to find a healthier balance between online and in-person interactions.

Do you check your phone every few minutes even when you are with your friends? One way is to measure the amount of time you spend online and compare it to the amount of time you spend with your friends in person. Challenge yourself to make your in-person time greater than your online time.

ROLE MODEL

At Level 1, a **ROLE MODEL** is defined as someone who possesses qualities that others admire, such as demonstrating respect for themselves and others. At Level 2, being a good role model revolves around modeling good behavior in school as well as on and off the field.

Good behavior starts with knowing the rules. In school, the rules usually include sitting still at your desk, listening to your teacher, and raising your hand if you want to speak. While some schools may have other rules, knowing—and obeying—those rules generally leads to good behavior.

On the field, good behavior starts with listening to your coaches, doing what they tell you, and not whining when things don't go your way. The best way to model good behavior on the field is to treat others the same way you would want them to treat you.

LIVING YOUR SPORT

Youth athletes who are serious about their chosen sport often cultivate a lifestyle in which they "live" the sport. At Level 1, youth baseball players demonstrate this attribute by playing simply for the love of the game. At Level 2, youth baseball players who live for the sport spend more time practicing drills and mastering skills. These are the boys who are often seen tossing a ball in the air and catching it wherever and whenever they can. They also begin to spend time watching professional baseball games live or on television to learn more about the game and observe the pros. Youth baseball players who live for the sport also start to spend more time learning the "unwritten rules" and understanding ALL the rules of the game.

HOW TO STUDY THE RULES OF BASEBALL »

Official Baseball Rules governs baseball games played by professional teams. The Official Playing Rules Committee is in charge of the rules, including making any changes to them. To read the latest version of *Official Baseball Rules*, go to Major League Baseball's website at www.mlb.com.

TREVOR HOFFMAN

Over the past decade or two, I have noticed an alarming trend of trying to force children to specialize in one sport—or even one position—as early as middle school. Coaches often urge this strategy, pointing to the importance of a player racking up great stats, standing out at showcases, and making the top travel ball leagues.

Parents often cave to the pressure, or are even the ones pushing for the specializations themselves because they believe that their son will fall behind his peers in terms of visibility to college coaches and professional scouts if he does not begin to focus on one position or skill set early on. The Number 1 priority of any coach and any parent should always be the health of the child; early specialization puts this at risk, as a young man's body is not yet developed enough to endure such focused training without running the risk of an overuse injury.

If there is one piece of advice I can offer coaches and parents at this level, it is that you resist the temptation to follow the specialization trend and simply let your son love the game… and even let him love other ones too if he is so inclined. If he isn't great at one sport, don't automatically pull him out to focus on one where he is better; give him a chance to explore and grow within the sport he finds more difficult if he wants.

One of the best sports experiences I had as a kid was playing basketball from junior high through high school. I was able to stay active during the offseason for baseball, and I came to love the pace and strategy of a different type of game.

Even though my brothers had both excelled at baseball and basketball, I never felt pressure from them or from my parents to follow in their footsteps.

The middle school years are also a great time for kids to spread their wings a bit and really start to come into their own as young people and as athletes. My older brothers were some of the most tremendous role models and sources of wisdom that I could have asked for as a child, but I also lived in their shadow. All the teachers and coaches had high hopes for the youngest Hoffman brother, which meant that I had a bit of a halo effect I could coast on.

When the middle school my brothers had attended closed, however, I ended up going to a different school with an all new set of teachers and coaches to whom I had to prove myself. On the one hand, I missed having that ready-made reputation, but it also meant that I had a clean slate, so I could decide to be whomever I wanted to be without feeling constrained or defined by other people's expectations. Junior high proved a really important opportunity for me to mature.

The role of siblings in a young person's development is so important. Whether being mentored by older siblings, as I was, or learning how to mentor younger siblings, family support is vital. Not only does a child have higher confidence and a sense of self-worth when he knows his entire family is behind him, but he also grows as he learns how to offer support and encouragement.

Even if a young athlete doesn't have any siblings, he can find that kind of support from cousins or very close friends. In my case, when I was in junior high, I was blessed to practice with the high school JV team coached by my oldest brother, Greg. I can't begin to describe how valuable it was for me to not only work on my skills against players older than me but also watch my older brother in a leadership position.

My brothers were also instrumental in teaching me how to keep a proper perspective on my sport. When I came home from Little League games, Greg would ask how I did. Immediately, I would launch into all of my statistics. He would ask again, "How did you do?" and again I would start rattling off how my at-bats had gone or what plays I had made in the infield. Inevitably, he would cut me off and say, "I meant 'you' as in your team. How did your team do? Always put the team first; that means more than your personal statistics."

My dad was such a strong, confident presence in our lives that my brothers learned at a young age how to be encouraging and available as well. They, in turn, modeled for me both how to show and how to earn respect as a young man—and those are lessons for which I will always be grateful.

JOIN THE CONVERSATION!

Download the **COMPLETE ATHLETE** app today for video updates and to connect with your team!

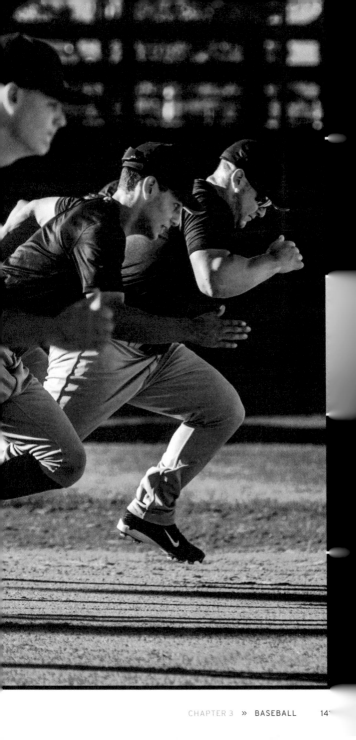

IN LEVEL 3

Athletes are starting to figure out what positions fit their strengths and how to make those strengths even more dynamic. Athletes are also learning how to keep their changing bodies healthy as the demands of the game increase. Parents are figuring out what steps they need to take to help their son be prepared for college, and how to explore options that might hopefully lead to a scholarship. Coaches carry a tremendous amount of influence as players navigate through the challenge of high school baseball and travel ball years.

3.1 ATTITUDE

A **POSITIVE ATTITUDE** is essential to an athlete's success both on and off the playing field, especially as he moves into higher levels of play. In fact, college coaches seek out athletes who display positive attitudes. A positive attitude is something that can be developed with practice, just like any other skill. A **COMPLETE ATHLETE** makes a habit of demonstrating the following five attributes:

RESPECT

SPORTSMANSHIP

TEAMWORK

PROFESSIONALISM

LEADERSHIP

BRENTON SULLIVAN >> *We survey college coaches and recruiters all the time, and they are looking beyond just athletic abilities. They are often wary of stats because they can be misleading due to factors such as level of competition. One factor that can help in the recruiting process is a high school coach who can vouch for an athlete's attitude and drive. He can talk to college recruiters about athletes who are leaders, who want to improve, and who will put in the hard work needed to succeed. College coaches are worried about chemistry. They know a problem player can impact an entire locker room. Talking to high school coaches about recruits' attitudes and work ethic can make a major difference in the recruiting process.*

RESPECT

Showing **RESPECT** means treating others in ways that show they have worth and value and being considerate of other people's feelings. Levels 1 and 2 discussed treating coaches and players with respect. At Level 3, a youth baseball player should work on treating himself with respect.

One of the most important ways to show yourself respect is by forgiving yourself if you make a mistake in the game. Mistakes happen to everyone. The time you spend dwelling on them is time and concentration you're taking away from other areas of your life. The most successful athletes have the ability to forget bad innings/games. Get over it and get right back into the game.

Respecting yourself also means taking good care of your physical body. As a youth athlete, you need to carefully nourish and hydrate your body according to the guidelines provided in this manual, not only for optimal performance on the field of play, but also for optimal health and well-being. In addition you must not be tempted to use performance-enhancing drugs or consume alcohol or other illegal substances.

ATHLETES >> "Obstacles are not in the way of your path; they are the path." One of our athletes was a top young pitcher who encountered the reality of the "business of college recruiting" in high school. He faced a difficult path as he tried to get into the elite level of college baseball.

As a freshman in high school, he was offered a scholarship and committed to a top Division I university.

You would have thought that allowed him to relax and no longer worry about the pressure of getting a scholarship, to focus instead on getting stronger and academics, but you would have been wrong.

This scholarship actually put a lot of pressure on him, especially as his body grew and changed during his high school years. These changes impacted his timing and coordination, which is important for any pitcher, and led to temporary velocity dips and inconsistency in the strike zone. His junior year was forgettable but not to the Division I university that originally gave him a scholarship. The program had to make a decision and didn't want to risk waiting to see if was better his senior year. The school took away his scholarship offer.

It was a devastating moment for his parents as well as the player. But he continued to work hard and respect the process. He knew he was far better than what he had showed in his junior year. Instead of dwelling on his problems, he went back to work and got better. By his senior year, his growing pains had slowed and he was pitching over 90 mph and became one of the top recruits in the country, even getting the attention of MLB scouts. He ended up going to another Division I university where he is doing well and very happy. With the right attitude and respect for the process, no matter what happens, the best players can stay on the right path despite the challenges they face. Adversity equals fuel.

SPORTSMANSHIP

Good **SPORTSMANSHIP** starts with respect for one's teammates, opponents, coaches, and officials. At Level 3, good sportsmanship is also demonstrated by players who maintain a positive attitude when dealing with adversity.

Accountability means taking responsibility for one's mistakes. In other words, if you make a mistake or bad play, you accept it; you do not make excuses for why it happened, and you do not blame others for it. In addition, when you know you've made a mistake, you accept the ruling on the field and do not argue with coaches or officials.

COACHES >> Sometimes, a pitcher is having a terrible day or is not on the same level as the opposing team. This can lead to lots of hits and runs, affecting the pitcher both physically and mentally. Sometimes, the coaches won't take the pitcher out, leaving him out there to dry.

On the flip side, the opposing team should not try to belittle or embarrass a pitcher. Running up the score on a pitcher looks trashy and reflects badly on a program. Always remember that situations change, and your team could be the one getting shelled in the future. "Say little when you lose, and say even less when you win" is something we tell our players, teaching them to be gracious when they win and when they lose.

TEAMWORK

TEAMWORK means working together as a group in order to achieve a goal. In sports, players contribute their individual skills and efforts in cooperation with their teammates to win games.

By Level 3, a youth baseball player is entering high school, and he may be feeling pressure to maximize his playing time to impress college recruiters. However, a baseball player who focuses more on his own individual performance instead of the team's performance will probably not impress very many recruiters.

ATHLETES >> Leadership can be something that finds you, often coming from circumstance rather than choice. One of our players, a hardworking and talented kid, never quite got the recognition he should have until he found himself in a difficult situation and learned how to be a team leader. He faced some adversity on and off the field and hadn't gotten any offer,s even though his stats proved him worthy. He and his family were worried about him getting in to college, and his senior year wasn't going exactly how he had envisioned it. However, like most challenges in life, if you keep working, things have a way of paying off.

During his senior year of high school, he played on a strong and talented team with very high expectations because of one very skilled player who was nationally ranked and likely to be drafted extremely high. But this player brought a lot of baggage that no amount of talent could hide. He had a major attitude problem and was a bully to lesser players. You hope your most talented players will also be your most humble, hardworking grinders, leading by example. This player was anything but that and bought into all the hype about how he was the "top ranked player in the area." He always had excuses for why he couldn't practice with the team and left early for different scout teams and meetings without giving the coach a heads-up. He didn't hustle, and he stayed in the dugout during batting practice when he should have been helping. He spent most of his time talking about all the great teams he was playing on, how much better that competition was, and his agent.

As the "baseball gods" would have it, this player got off to a slow start, and the team struggled at the beginning of the season. He began moping around, sitting in the dugout more, and doing even less to help out with batting practice or field cleanup. His bad attitude impacted the rest of the team, bringing the other players down. It was only a matter of time before it came to a head, and our player, the one who was hard-working and liked by the team, finally called out this player on his behavior. It got ugly and almost turned into a physical fight, but the cocky, arrogant player backed down quickly like most bullies do.

The team came together after this and found a new leader to rally around. They really gelled and played well. It is important for a team to recognize early if a certain player is causing poor team chemistry. If you do not fix the issue early, it can become a major problem and ruin a season.

If one-on-one conversation doesn't work, you can mention to your coach that you and others players are worried about a potential issue with a teammate. Although this team waited and let the situation get bad, at least it was finally addressed rather than avoided. Our player went on to get a scholarship and is continuing his path to play pro ball in the future. The other player wasn't drafted and was released from his scholarship in the fall of his freshman year. A large reason for the turnaround was this act of leadership and getting the team behind him.

PROFESSIONALISM

Certainly a youth athlete is not a **PROFESSIONAL** in the sense of being paid to play. However, developing the attitude and behaviors of a professional can help him more easily move up through the levels.

At Level 2, a youth baseball player begins to take responsibility for keeping his uniform and equipment clean and well-maintained, for maintaining his personal hygiene, and for arriving at practices and games well-groomed and ready to go to work.

At Level 3, this responsibility takes on even more importance as college recruiters visit high schools to watch teams play. Players who display a professional appearance and demeanor will definitely make a good impression on recruiters.

BRENTON SULLIVAN >> *High school athletes looking to play college ball need to stand out. They often try to get exposure by going to camps and showcases, bombarding college coaches' offices with letters, emails, DVDs, video* clips, and any anything else to get on their radar. But, in reality, recruiting doesn't work that way as tens of thousands of other athletes are doing the same thing.

One of the best ways to stand out is for a high school athlete to take a coach-centric recruiting approach. Coaches know each other and have networked over the years. High school coaches have spent years building their own reputations. They aren't going to ruin them with college recruiters by talking up players who don't have the talent to perform at the college level. High school athletes should assemble a list of colleges they want to target and share it with their high school coaches. It's very possible the high school coach knows someone who works for or is affiliated with one of the programs on the list. If that's the case, the coach can make a call on the athlete's behalf. Their chances of getting through are far better than a parent or a high school athlete making that call.

LEADERSHIP

A good **LEADER** is a "connector," able to inspire and motivate others to do something that they would not normally do or perform better than they would on their own. A youth baseball player can sometimes motivate and inspire his fellow players in ways that coaches cannot.

As a youth baseball player enters high school at Level 3, he should continue to develop his leadership skills through his interactions with teammates. In fact, he may decide he's ready to take his skills to the next level by becoming a team leader.

A team leader needs to have the trust and respect of his teammates in order to be effective. One way to earn that trust and respect is to encourage players to come to him with questions, to bounce off ideas, or even to complain. As his teammates' confidence in him grows, he can help strengthen the team through team-building and problem-solving activities.

ATHLETES >> A recent example of leadership that I have witnessed was from Ryan Rodriguez, a baseball player from my hometown who was recruited by and eventually signed his letter of intent with the University of California-Davis. In the city of Upland, there is a really neat baseball field called Memorial Park that used to be a wonderful and safe community hangout. In recent years, however, it had started to attract transients and fallen into neglect. The situation got so bad that, when games were played there, an adult escort was required for anyone to use the public restrooms at the field because the facilities had become so dangerous.

Ryan Rodriguez, while he was still in high school, went of his own accord to Upland City Hall and presented the situation to the city council. He asked what steps needed to be taken to clean up the field and resolve the safety situations. He didn't make a big deal about it, but it had a major impact. There was an article about it in the paper and a huge response from the community. The city responded to this support and shut down the field for several days to clean it up and move the homeless people using it as a camp into shelters.

I was so impressed by the leadership of that young man to recognize the situation, resolve to do something about it, and rally people together for the cause. He set such an outstanding example to younger players to show them that they have a voice and can make positive changes too.

COACH MIKE MARTIN » *If a potential recruit makes poor decisions that show a real lack of character, we're going to get off of him. I don't want someone like that to come in here because it gives us a little bit of a reputation as a program that takes people who might influence others in the wrong direction. We're not going to take every single good player, but we're going to go after every single good player of good character who we see as doing the best he can do in the classroom.*

JOIN THE CONVERSATION!
Follow and chat with your coach and teammates in the **COMPLETE ATHLETE** app!

3.2 PREPARATION

As we discussed in Levels 1 and 2, **PREPARATION** refers to off-field activities, such as practicing skills, eating right, staying hydrated, getting enough rest, and mentally preparing for a game or practice. Coaches love athletes who prepare: These are the players who are eager to learn, eager to play, and ultimately, eager to win. They are the athletes that coaches want to help succeed because they already have a winning attitude. Preparation also helps athletes feel positive and confident in their ability to perform.

A **COMPLETE ATHLETE** prepares to perform on the field of play by continuously improving on the following:

PRACTICE

NUTRITION

HYDRATION

RECOVERY

MENTALITY

PRACTICE

A youth athlete who has surpassed Level 2 obviously considers baseball a huge part of his life. By this point, he should have already begun to work with a private baseball coach or spent more time on his own to master the basic techniques and begin to learn a few position-specific skills.

At Level 3, a youth athlete should begin to identify positions at which he is most proficient. Both his team's coaches and his private coach can help him decide which positions make the most sense for him. In addition to team **PRACTICES** and one-on-one sessions with his private coach, the youth baseball player can continue his regular individual practice sessions, focusing extra attention on the skills needed for the positions he wants to play.

One additional note: College coaches look for—and recruit—players who contribute the most. The more proficient a player is at multiple positions, the more game time he will get.

ATHLETES » I grew up close to a nice park where there were many large old trees with giant branches extending all over the place. All of these branches provided an aerial obstacle course with tight lanes to navigate around. I would watch a huge hawk that lived in one of the trees soar low through the park, flying through the trees and between the branches. This got me wondering how I could use this for throwing baseballs or footballs through and around the trees. By doing so, I could work on eliminating outside objects and focus on my target.

I would go down to the park almost every day with two footballs. Throwing a football gets baseball players stronger and helps them find a more efficient arm path when they throw. At the park, I would drop back and pretend I was playing quarterback, throwing the ball to the different trees, seeing how accurate I was.

Doing this helped my baseball career because it increased my arm strength and got me better at eliminating things that weren't in my path. Later on, as a coach, I would bring players down to the park to work on throwing. I used to have Chad Hockins, who played third base and was the closer for Cal State Fullerton and is now with the Cubs, go to the same park and throw through the gaps in the trees to improve his accuracy. He looked at me as though I was kind of strange when he first heard it, but he learned to love it as much as I did.

JON OLSEN » *I had a lot of success early on, but then an injury took me out of the game my junior and senior years of high school. Everyone thought I would go really high in the draft, but I didn't because I had fallen behind while I was recovering. Instead of going straight to the pros, I was recruited to UCLA, and that proved to be a great move for me. I'm still not all the way back to where I want to be, but in a strange way, I am grateful for that injury because it forced me to learn self-discipline and how to deal with adversity, both of which are essential for success.*

If you get back from a game at 2:30 AM, you have to be ready to be up at 7 AM to work out. You have to be willing to put in the effort and not just rest on your laurels. Some athletes never face any challenges early on, and when they inevitably end up facing them later, many of them don't know how to handle it. The earlier you learn how to manage the stressors and develop self-discipline, the better. It needs to start before you are off on your own in college or the pros.

For me, that injury in high school ended up being a good thing because I am really happy with where I am right now. But I also know where I want to be, so I am going to keep working to get there!

NUTRITION

As a youth baseball player enters high school, nutrition continues to play a key role in his life. Nutrition is important not only for optimal performance on the field of play but also to obtain the vitamins and minerals needed for optimal health.

LEVEL-3 ATHLETE NUTRITION GUIDELINES >>

Each individual has different macronutrient needs, based on height, weight, age, activity level, and genetic background. The following macronutrient guidelines are based on age and estimated activity level for a Level 3 athlete:

- 50 percent carbohydrate
- 25 percent protein
- 25 percent fat
- No more than 7 percent saturated fat
- No trans fat
- 38 grams of fiber per day
- No more than 150 calories per day from sugar (37.5 grams or 9 teaspoons)

ATHLETES >> Daniel Robertson was an elite high school player preparing for his senior year, which was expected to be big because of how high he was projected to go in the upcoming MLB Draft. We were training him extremely hard, just as we had been the last three or four years.

He had reached a plateau with his weight, but he was still strong and making personal bests in all his lifts and speed tests. However, he wasn't gaining weight as he should have. So he focused on adding more protein, using some over-the-counter protein drink and trying different methods suggested by others. Nothing seemed to work though. His parents decided to take him to a dietitian and nutritionist. They did a blood test, which showed that there were certain proteins from generic over-the-counter protein shakes he was drinking that his body was rejecting. He was given very thorough information on what to eat and what to avoid. Certain proteins were better than others.

Once he knew this, he adjusted his diet and became much stronger. He had more energy and even grew more confident. Sure enough, he had an outstanding year and ended up drafted higher than expected, becoming a millionaire at the age of 18. Don't just assume that your lack of strength and size gains are a work ethic problem or an exercise choice, it may take more digging to find that perfect formula to get those gains. He did extensive work, more than most kids would have, but it paid off.

PARENTS >> Some showcases at this level might have an 8 AM check-in, but these can still be long days. Despite the early check-ins, pitchers might not start until after lunch, something players and their families might not know until they arrive. Typically at a showcase, position players start running their 60-yard dashes, testing their arms, and working on batting practice while pitchers are just standing around waiting all day. As they wait, pitchers get stiff and lethargic. Families should be prepared for a long day, and that means thinking about food. Scout out the area; find healthy options to get good food for fuel. Perhaps even ask about the schedule for pitchers and if it is necessary to check in hours before he is going to pitch.

One time, after a player had a great showcase, his parents told me he spent most of the day waiting, but because they had done their homework, they knew a place around the corner that had smoothies and healthy sandwiches. Because he had a better lunch than the other players, he had more energy when it was time to show his stuff.

HYDRATION

If an athlete does not drink enough water, he could suffer from dehydration. Warning signs of dehydration include the following:

- Thirst
- Irritability
- Headaches
- Weakness
- Dizziness
- Cramps
- Nausea
- Increased risk of injury

JOIN THE CONVERSATION!

Don't miss out on additional tips on recovery and proper hydration from coaches and professionals in the **COMPLETE ATHLETE** app!

HOW TO MAINTAIN PROPER HYDRATION* >>

- Before exercise, drink 16 to 20 full ounces within the two-hour period prior to exercise.
- During exercise, drink 4 to 6 full ounces.
- After exercise, replace 24 full ounces for every one pound of body weight lost during exercise.

RECOVERY

Youth baseball players need to eat and drink within 30 minutes of a practice or game to make up for calories they are burning and fluids they are using. Replenishing calories and fluids also aids in muscle recovery and repair.

HOW TO REPLENISH CALORIES AND FLUIDS >>

- Drink 24 ounces of fluid for every pound of sweat lost within two hours of a game or practice.
- Consume 20 to 25 grams of protein plus an equal amount of carbohydrates within the 30-minute recovery window.

SLEEP >>

An athlete's body does its growing, healing, and muscle repair during sleep. A high school athlete may still be going through a growth spurt; therefore, sleep is crucial for proper growth and development. According to the National Sleep Foundation, a Level 3 youth athlete should get 8 to 10 hours of sleep each night for proper growth and development.

―――――――

* *Adapted from guidelines provided by the American College of Sports Medicine (ACSM)*

A lot of youth baseball players stress out about the amount of sleep they are getting, especially the night before a big game. It's best not to put too much emphasis on the quality of your sleep the night before game day because anticipation and excitement can cause restless sleep. Instead, consider the most important night of sleep to be two days before game day, and the second to be three days before game day. Make sure you get the sleep you need on those nights, and try to rest before the actual game on game day.

ATHLETES >> One of our high school athletes, an under-classman, was an impressive lefty who was asked to play on an elite travel ball team that played in tournaments across the nation. The team flew him out to one, making it the first time he had ever traveled by himself and stayed in his own hotel room. However, he wound up not playing because he slept through the alarm clock after turning it off when he meant to hit the snooze button. As a new player on an elite team, he had blown his chance to shine.

This served as a big wake-up call for this player. He realized he needed to take more responsibility and wake up and get ready on his own no matter how early. Granted, this player learned his lesson, and he committed to a Division I school a year later. His grades have gotten higher and his attitude, work ethic, most everything, have gotten better. While it was a bad experience, he learned and grew from it.

MENTALITY

Being a better athlete does not necessarily mean training harder or longer.

Certainly, a youth baseball player must spend time physically preparing his body to meet the demands of a practice session or game. Similarly, engaging in mental preparation can help him perform at a higher level by creating the proper mindset for either a practice or game.

To be successful in any sport, athletes must apply 100 percent of their energy and thoughts toward each activity. In other words, they need to have their "heads in the game." At Level 3, youth baseball players should work on staying focused.

HOW TO IMPROVE YOUR FOCUS »

The following suggestions are adapted from *Sports Psychology for Dummies* by Leif H. Smith and Todd M. Kays.

KNOW WHAT YOU NEED TO FOCUS ON. The clearer you are about what you want to focus on, the more likely you'll be to stay focused on the factors that contribute to your success.

FOCUS ON WHAT YOU CAN CONTROL. You have control over yourself and your own actions and attitudes—nothing more. Keep your focus here. If you focus on outcomes (things you have no control over), you're creating unnecessary anxiety. Focus on the process and you increase the likelihood of positive results happening.

STAY RELAXED UNDER PRESSURE. When you're stressed and anxious, your focus drops. Find ways to stay calm in high-pressure situations. Take deep breaths, stretch muscles to loosen them, or engage in effective routines to keep your focus where it needs to be.

USE CUE WORDS. Cue words are simple words and phrases that remind you of your focus points. Repeating words and phrases such as relax, play hard, or quick feet will remind you to focus on what you need to do. If your mind is focused on your cue words, your body will follow.

ATHLETES » Moving into my senior year of high school, I had a coach who suggested we take up mental practice. I had not thought about mental practice before, but it would come to help me a great deal. Our coach gave us audiotapes by Ken Ravizza, a renowned sport psychologist out of Cal State Fullerton who has worked with both the Angels and Rays. I vividly remember going home and listening to the tapes. Each night before I pitched, I would listen to his voice. He would go over things, giving me breathing exercises and examples.

He would say, "Put the hay in the barn. You've been working hard. You've harvested the hay. Now it's time to put it in the barn and start to enjoy the labor of it." It might sound weird, but it has stayed with me to this day. I even use that story to tell kids why it's important to go out and find audio clips or read things—from books to blogs—to learn about mental practice. At this level, it can be the edge that makes you better than the competition.

PARENTS/ATHLETES >> The right mentality can make all the difference in being successful in baseball and in life. I have had countless conversations with families and athletes who think their present situation may lead to the end of their chances of playing baseball past high school. I remember once sitting in my office and getting ready to head out to the field.

One of my athletes came in with his parents, and they looked as though someone had just given them the worst news they could possibly hear. I asked what was wrong. The mother jumped in and told me their son didn't make varsity. I said, "So what? That's great news!"

All three looked at me kind of puzzled. I explained to them to look at the big picture and see the positives. I said, "Your son is only a sophomore and now can have much more time devoted to training outside of practice. Most JV programs don't intimidate you or question why you are getting more instruction outside of the high school program."

This was very important for this athlete, and his face lit up along with his parents. You could see a major change in his attitude as he saw right away the possibilities and benefits of getting to work on improving his weaknesses and making his strengths even greater.

A positive attitude can be hard to keep when so many things and people seem to be negative in and around baseball, but we have to remember that the journey to reach your dreams is not always laid out exactly how you planned. That attitude will prepare you to handle things in life so much better. I even like to point out that some of my best players who have gone on to play professional baseball didn't even make varsity until their senior year.

A few didn't even play that much during that year. But they used the disappointment as motivation to prove those coaches wrong and prove the people who believed in them right. Also, it's good to know that some pretty impressive Hall of Fame and future Hall of Fame players were not recruited to four-year schools and attended junior college before making it to the MLB. Take a look at these names: Albert Pujols, Curt Schilling, Andy Pettitte, Kirby Puckett, Mike Piazza, Bryce Harper, and even Jackie Robinson. A strong positive attitude can get you through some of the darker days and turn that adversity into fuel.

3.3 FITNESS

FITNESS matters. Strength and speed are required to play the game of baseball effectively. Flexibility and mobility help to prevent injuries. As a youth baseball player reaches Level 3, he begins to separate himself from other players by demonstrating a serious dedication to his own personal fitness. This helps not only does to establish a foundation of strength but also teaches good habits needed for success in higher levels of baseball. After all, the demands of training at the college and pro levels can be mentally and physically challenging, especially for those lower-level athletes who are not already used to working that hard.

LOWER-BODY STRENGTH

UPPER-BODY STRENGTH

FLEXIBILITY / MOBILITY

CORE STRENGTH

SPEED / QUICKNESS / ENDURANCE

LOWER-BODY STRENGTH

The demands to maintain your fitness and health during practice and games can depend on your leg strength. We know stronger legs can make you run faster and throw harder, but they also allow you to be more explosive at your positions—catching balls in the gap, making plays in the hole, or driving big-time fastballs past hitters.

A strong, fit lower-body is the foundation for staying healthy and the ability to absorb the pounding of tough practices or long seasons. You will still be tested and should show improvement with the single-leg squat and lateral jump, but we have added the vertical test now, which will test your power to jump high. It is the standard coaches use to test your athleticism and see if you have power in your legs. Colleges want to see athletes with powerful jumping ability. When an athlete has equal strength in both legs, he will produce higher scores.

TO PERFORM SINGLE-LEG SQUATS >>

- Stand on one leg while the other leg is lifted off the ground in front of the body. The hip should be bent to approximately 45 degrees and the knee bent to approximately 90 degrees.
- Hold the arms out straight in front of you with the hands clasped together. From this position, squat down until the knee is bent to approximately 60 degrees.
- Return to the start position and repeat.

TO PERFORM A VERTICAL JUMP »

- Stand next to wall and reach as high as you can without lifting your toes or heel off the ground.
- Measure that distance from the ground.
- Stand away from the wall, jump as high as you can, and touch the wall.
- Measure the distance between standing reach height and jump height.

TO PERFORM A LATERAL JUMP »

- Stand on one leg with the foot at the starting line and hands on hips.
- Squat down quickly and then jump sideways as far as possible, landing on both feet without losing balance.
- Measure the distance jumped to the nearest foot.

UPPER-BODY STRENGTH

Boys are older and players are getting stronger. You need to stay ahead of the curve to make sure you can hit the ball harder and throw farther than your competition. At this age, we see a lot of bodies that haven't yet hit full puberty and lack the size of other athletes. This doesn't mean the others are stronger. I have seen smaller athletes who work hard in the gym and are much more athletic and stronger because of it. Size comes later.

To do well at these tests and see improvement, you need to get in the weight room and put an emphasis on upper-body exercises. In highly competitive levels such as high school and travel ball, these may give you an edge over other athletes and grab the attention of college recruiters.

In Levels 1 and 2, **UPPER-BODY STRENGTH** was identified as an important element for good baseball fitness. Exercises that improve the strength and mobility of the upper-body muscles help a baseball player throw faster and farther. Improving the strength and mobility of the upper-body decelerator muscles is important for safe deceleration during throwing actions. This is especially important for pitchers, who throw the ball more often than other position players.

TO PERFORM A VERTICAL PULL-UP »

- Grasp an overhead bar using the neutral grip or underhand grip (palms facing toward body), arms fully extended and legs hanging straight down.
- Raise the body up until the chin clears the top of the bar.
- Lower again to the starting position, arms again fully extended.

TO PERFORM PUSH-UPS >>

- Lie facedown on the floor (or mat) with hands under the shoulders or slightly wider than the chest, fingers straight, legs straight and parallel.
- Straighten the arms, pushing the upper-body up and keeping the back and knees straight.
- Bend the arms to lower the upper-body until the elbows are at a 90-degree angle and the upper arms are parallel to the floor.
- Perform as many repetitions as possible without resting.

TO PERFORM A SITTING MEDICINE BALL THROW >>

- Sit on the floor with back against a wall and legs fully extended (about 2 feet apart).
- Hold a 5-pound medicine ball with hands on the side and slightly behind the center. Place back of ball against the center of the chest. Forearms should be parallel to the ground.
- Throw the medicine ball vigorously straightforward as far as possible while keeping back against the wall.
- Record the distance thrown.

Rotational medicine ball throws follow the same motor pattern used in games. They help to teach youth baseball players how to transfer power from rotational movements such as swinging and throwing. It may be the single most important component in training to hit and throw harder.

TO PERFORM A ROTATIONAL MEDICINE BALL THROW

- Stand perpendicular to a start line (such as in a pitching or hitting stance).
- Hold a medicine ball in both hands, placing back hand

on the back of the ball and the front hand under the ball.
- Draw the ball back with only a slight bend at the elbows, keeping the ball between the waist and chest.
- In one swift motion, fling the ball up and forward (optimally at a 45-degree angle).

FLEXIBILITY / MOBILITY

A good degree of **FLEXIBILITY** and **MOBILITY** leads to better baseball technique and helps to prevent injuries. As discussed in Level 1 and 2, the sit-and-reach test is used to assess—and improve—a youth athlete's level of lower-body flexibility and mobility. Likewise, the shoulder-stretch test is used to assess and improve a youth athlete's level of upper-body flexibility and mobility.

TO PERFORM THE SIT-AND-REACH TEST »

NOTE » You'll need a box that is 12 inches high, such as a milk crate. Tape a yardstick or ruler to the top so that the first 9 inches hang over the edge and the 9-inch mark is exactly on the edge against which you will place your feet.

- Place the box against a wall.
- Sit on the floor in front of the box with your legs straight in front of you and the soles of your feet flat against the front side of the box. (The overhanging part of the ruler should be pointed at your chest or midsection.)
- Keeping the legs straight and flat on the floor, stretch forward and reach along the ruler with one hand on top of the other, palms down.
- Stretch forward three times without bouncing; then reach as far as possible, holding at the farthest point for at least three seconds.

TO PERFORM THE SHOULDER-STRETCH TEST >>

- Stand with feet slightly apart.
- Place one hand behind the head and back over the shoulder with the palm touching your body and fingers directed downward.
- Place the other arm behind your back, palm facing outward and fingers upward.
- Reach as far as possible, attempting to touch the fingers of each hand together.
- Repeat with the other side.

CORE STRENGTH

Building up your **CORE STRENGTH** can be a game changer for an athlete who is competing on top travel teams or trying to break into his high school's starting lineup. Don't forget that the core is quite literally the glue to your body's "engine" for acceleration and deceleration. It allows the larger prime moving muscles to convert energy into whatever athletic move you are going to make, whether throwing a ball or simply reacting to a hit ball and making an incredible catch. Strong core muscles are of huge importance because of the added speed and power to your swing or throw. Remember, as you get older higher velocities are achieved, which means higher stress to the body. A strong core is your protection from injury.

TO PERFORM A PLANK >>

- Get down on the floor with your hands apart slightly wider than shoulder-width, your arms straight and supporting your weight.
- Make sure your body stays straight. Your hips shouldn't be sticking way up in the air or sagging.
- Hold that position as long as you can.

TO PERFORM A SIDE PLANK >>

- Lie on your side with your legs straight.
- Prop up your upper-body on your elbow and forearm. (Make sure your elbow is aligned with the shoulder.)
- Brace your core by contracting your abs forcefully, and then raise your hips until your body forms a straight line from your ankles to your shoulders.
- Breathe deeply while holding this position.
- Repeat this exercise on your other side.

The **HIP-LIFT MARCH** helps to measure and improve the strength and endurance of the back muscles.

TO PERFORM A HIP-LIFT MARCH >>

- Lie flat on your back, knees bent 90 degrees and feet flat on the ground.
- Lift hips as high as possible; only shoulders and feet should touch the ground.
- Keeping hips at the same height, lift each knee in a controlled marching motion for as long as possible.

SPEED/QUICKNESS/ENDURANCE

As discussed in Levels 1 and 2, there are two types of baseball speed:

- Straightaway speed on the base paths or in the outfield
- Lateral (side-to-side) quickness, such as when an infielder moves to get a ground ball

The 30-yard sprint helps an athlete improve straightaway speed. The 5-10-5 Shuttle Run, or Pro Agility Drill, is a great way to improve lateral quickness because it helps to hone an athlete's ability to accelerate, decelerate, stop, and reaccelerate without losing balance. The Beep Test is a good way to measure and improve endurance.

TO PERFORM A 5-10-5 SHUTTLE RUN >>

- Set up three marker cones 5 yards apart.
- Start at the middle marker cone in a three-point stance.
- Turn and run 5 yards to the right side and touch the marker cone with the right hand.

- Turn around and run 10 yards to the left and touch the marker cone with the left hand.
- Finish by running back to the middle marker cone.

TO PERFORM A 30-YARD SPRINT »

- Place two cones 30 yards apart.
- Starting at one cone, run as fast as you can to the other cone.

TO PERFORM A BEEP TEST »

NOTE » You'll first need to download a Beep Test audio recording or Beep Test app, which will play beeps at set intervals. As the test proceeds, the interval between each successive beep reduces, forcing the athlete to increase his speed.

- Draw two lines 40 yards apart.
- Stand behind one of the lines, face the second line, and begin running when instructed by the recording.
- Continue running between the two lines, turning when signaled by the recorded beeps. After about one minute, a sound indicates an increase in speed, and the beeps will be closer together.
- The test is stopped when the athlete can no longer keep in sync with the recording.

JOIN THE CONVERSATION!

Fitness is key to performance. Get more tips and how-to's in the **COMPLETE ATHLETE** app.

LEVEL-3 FITNESS TEST

LOWER-BODY STRENGTH
- Five full-range single-leg squats with each leg
- Vertical jump of 20 inches or greater
- Lateral jump of 85 inches or greater

UPPER-BODY STRENGTH
- 10 pull-ups for position plays, 8 for pitchers
- 35 push-ups in 60 seconds for position players, 30 for pitchers
- Sitting medicine ball throw of at least 12 feet
- Rotational medicine ball throw of at least 40 feet with an 8-pound ball

FLEXIBILITY/MOBILITY
- At least 35 centimeters in the sit-and-reach test
- Shoulder-stretch test (pass or fail)

CORE STRENGTH
- 3-minute plank
- 50-second side plank on each side
- Hip-lift march with perfect form for 2 minutes
- Balance 30 seconds on each leg

SPEED/QUICKNESS/ENDURANCE
- 5-10-5 Shuttle Run in 5 seconds
- 30-yard sprint in 4.2 seconds for position players, 4.4 seconds for pitchers
- Beep Test minimum score of Level 8

3.4 TECHNIQUE

In just about any sport, the basic **TECHNIQUES** are the most important skills to master. These skills are the building blocks upon which more advanced skills are learned. Although you might have started to specialize in a specific position at Level 2, at Level 3 you will spend the majority of your private practice time in the position you (or your coaches) feel you will play at the next level. If you're serious about succeeding at higher levels of baseball, professional instruction is highly recommended.

Remember, a **COMPLETE ATHLETE** not only masters the basic and advanced skills needed to play the game of baseball but also understands the roles and responsibilities of every position on a team and how all the positions work together to win games. The basic skills of baseball include the following:

THROWING

HITTING

INFIELD FIELDING

OUTFIELD FIELDING

GAME ASSESSMENT

THROWING

Good **THROWING** technique requires accuracy, arm strength, and proper mechanics to make plays and gain the attention of college recruiters. I have seen players with all things equal in the classroom and stat book, but the one who has sound, clean mechanics will be the one the coach wants on his roster. Coaches have limited time to instruct in college, so they are looking for polished deliveries. At Level 3, technique does not change, but accuracy and strength will need to increase at all positions:

INFIELDERS must be able to throw accurately, both on the run and with their bodies in odd or unbalanced positions. Additionally, ball exchanges have to be quicker without sacrificing strength and accuracy.

OUTFIELDERS must cover more ground, and out-of-glove exchanges must be quicker without sacrificing strength and accuracy.

PITCHERS need to throw 65 percent strikes and command off-speed pitches at the same ratio during games. They must also field their position and make accurate throws to bases (PFP or Pitching Fielding Practice).

CATCHERS must be able to throw accurately to bases. Pop time to second base should be 2.05 seconds or under. They also must be able to keep the ball in the strike zone and keep balls thrown in the dirt in front of them.

HITTING

At Level 2, baseball players adjusted to **HITTING** in larger fields. At Level 3, players must learn to perform situational hitting. This requires the ability to recognize curve balls, sliders, change-ups, and fastballs. It also requires awareness of the game situation: Allowing a runner to get from third base to home plate, moving a runner over to the next base by hitting a bunt, placing a ground ball on the right side, or executing a slash contact swing.

COMMON MISTAKES >>

- Pulling off fastballs/curveballs/change-ups
- Getting front foot down late
- Long, loopy swings
- Drifting
- Hooking the ball or not going with pitch location

INFIELD FIELDING

College evaluators will scrutinize **INFIELD FIELDING**, and they will be looking for small details in your play.

It could be in your setup, approach to the ball, exchange, or footwork. It is important to practice as much as you can and have a professional teach you finer points that you may be lacking. Recruiters also want to see if you can play multiple positions, so practice taking ground balls from all over the infield.

COMMON MISTAKES >>

- Getting down too late
- Poor body positioning
- Bringing eyes up too soon
- Waiting on the ball to get to you
- Unwillingness to play new positions

DIFFERENT POSITIONS REQUIRE DIFFERENT SKILLS

PITCHERS

- Avoid overthrowing.
- Keep pitch counts low and build arm back up at new distance.
- Develop smart pitch selection.
- Learn to control the running game.

CATCHERS

- Keep received balls in the strike zone.
- Be able to block three out of five balls in the dirt within a 2-foot radius of your knees.
- Stay on your toes and be ready to move with runners on base.
- Control the running game by calling smart pitches and learning to block balls.

COMMON MISTAKES »

• Being out of position or too deep
• Sloppy footwork before ball gets to glove
• Staying back on balls hit to you

OUTFIELD FIELDING

The main activity in **OUTFIELD FIELDING** is catching fly balls and throwing them to the infield. An outfielder must be able to catch while running to the left, to the right, backward, and forward. He must also be able to throw the ball quickly and accurately. Outfielders also need to be ready in case grounders escape the infield.

COMMON MISTAKES »

• Late reaction to hit balls
• Poor body position when catching the ball
• Missing cutoffs
• Poor communication with other position players

GAME ASSESSMENT

GAME ASSESSMENT refers to the ability to perform the above techniques during the demands of an actual game, not just in practice. It also includes developing good judgment regarding in-game decisions. Game assessment is summarized below:

• Making accurate throws
• Ability to forget about bad at-bats or plays, which may affect future plays/at-bats

- Fielding your position properly
- Making good contact off live pitches
- Making smart base-running decisions
- When pitching, throwing strikes at least 60 percent of the time
- Backing up other outfielders and bases
- Anticipating where the ball may be hit by knowing what pitch is being thrown (and what the hitter may do with it)
- Hitting your cutoff man 100 percent of the time

COMMON MISTAKES >>

- Poor decisions on where to throw balls
- Getting thrown out often at bases
- Poor execution of situational hitting
- Pitchers making too many mistakes: giving up two strike hits, walks, especially leadoff walks
- Catchers giving up pass balls frequently
- Overthrowing bases
- Taking balls out of the strike zone

MLB PITCHER >> *I was drafted out of high school as a catcher. But, when I went to college, I became a two-way player. I ended up just pitching. That wasn't that big a transition for me since I had been doing it my whole life.*

But knowing more than one position has helped during my career. It's crucial for everyone to know every position. When I was in high school, my coach made it a point for all of us to know every position even if we didn't play it. I might not have ever played second base but I knew what the second baseman's responsibilities were on every single play. It was a good reminder that everyone had a job to do.

This has helped me to this day, letting me know where I have to be and where everyone else is. Sometimes, pitchers feel like they don't have a job to do after the ball is thrown and after it's hit. Being a catcher and playing other positions made it easier to comprehend the other jobs.

LEVEL-3 SKILLS TEST

To pass Level 3 Technique, a youth baseball player must be able to perform the following:

THROWING »

• A player should be able to throw the ball at least 250 feet five times within six-foot radius of the target.

POSITION SPECIFIC »

OUTFIELDERS Throw accurately five times from a minimum distance of 150 feet, or from right field to third base and right field to home within a six-foot radius of the target.

NOTE » The thrown ball should not have a high arc.

SUGGESTION » Place a coach or player in a cutoff position for testing to determine accuracy.

INFIELDERS Throw accurately five times in a row from deep shortstop. Also moving to your left side and throwing accurately five times in a row.

PITCHERS Throw strikes 65 percent of the time with fastballs, change-ups, and curveballs.

CATCHERS Throw three out of five balls to second base in 2.05 seconds or less.

HITTING >>

- Hit line drives off the tee to all fields (left/center/right) five times in a row.
- Hit the ball seven times in a row to all fields from a soft toss.

NOTE >> Coach should place balls in areas that will make the batter hit the ball where it is pitched, i.e., inside pitches should be pulled, balls thrown outside should be hit opposite field, and balls down the middle should be hit to center field.

Off live pitching, execute the following:

- Situational hitting
- 3 out of 3 bunts
- 3 out of 3 slash hits
- 3 out of 3 attempts to move a runner with a ground ball on the right side
- 3 out of 3 attempts to bring a runner in from third base with a fly ball.
- If at any time the ball pops up or is missed, start over.

INFIELD FIELDING >>

- Catch 10 ground balls consecutively cleanly hit to you from a coach.

NOTE >> Alternate from forehand to backhand while running forward and straight. The athlete should get 4 seconds after catching the ball to reset.

SUGGESTION >> Set up cones 10 yards apart with the player in the middle.

The coach should hit each ball toward the cones, both backhand and forehand.

• Demonstrate the ability to catch pop-ups. Make five quick, clean exchanges with accurate throws to target.

• Range test: Cover 10 yards in 1.1 seconds.

OUTFIELD FIELDING >>

NOTE >> Set up a circle with a 20-yard radius in the outfield. Have the player stand in the center in a ready position. The coach will throw one ball at a time to alternating areas of the circle. Once the ball is caught, allow the player 6 seconds to return and reset. Catch all 10 within the time.

• Catch the ball hit to you five times consecutively.

NOTE >> Balls should be hit with a height that requires an outfielder to move and catch on the run or set up properly to catch a fly ball.

• Make five consecutive catches thrown from the coach.

NOTE >> These balls should be similar to line drives. Catches should be made while running from either direction without losing stride.

TWO-BALL CATCH DRILL >>

An outfielder runs from one cone in a straight line away from the coach. The coach throws one ball over the player's right shoulder and the second ball over his left shoulder as he catches first ball.

Outfielder must do three sets perfectly without drops. Allow 15 seconds to return to original line between each set. Cones should be 30 yards apart. Cleanly field five balls hit on the ground and exchange out of glove with accurate throwing technique.

To pass Level 3 Game Assessment, a coach must assess each player as follows:

POSITION PLAYERS situational hitting, smart defensive plays and instincts, fielding, and base running.

PITCHERS getting ahead of hitters, executing pitches, hitting spots, defending his position

CATCHERS setting up, blocking, managing the running game, calling pitches.

3.5 LIFESTYLE

As youth baseball players achieve higher levels of success, they will find the demands on their time increasing. Creating a healthy balance between sports, academics, family obligations, and social activities requires strong time-management skills and a clear understanding of what's important.

As a youth baseball player moves into Level 3 during his high school years, he will shift the way he balances those elements in his life as he and his family begin to focus on getting into college and earning scholarships.

FAMILY

ACADEMICS

SOCIAL LIFE

ROLE MODEL

LIVING YOUR SPORT

FAMILY

College coaches want mature, respectful student-athletes as part of their program. During school visits, many observe how prospects treat their parents. Baseball players who have worked hard to maintain positive relationships within their families will definitely stand out.

At Levels 1 and 2, a youth baseball player's parents take on a fair amount of responsibility.

At Level 3, parents are probably spending a great deal more money for baseball, purchasing better equipment, private coaching sessions, and more. They are also likely devoting even more of their time to support their son's desire to excel in baseball.

As a youth baseball player moves into more serious levels of play, he should begin to assume more responsibility for baseball activities. This helps the baseball player learn to be independent and self-sufficient, two traits that he will need to be successful in college.

HOW TO BECOME MORE INDEPENDENT AND SELF-SUFFICIENT »

- Always remember all your parents do to support you and be grateful. Never take your parents for granted.
- Try to be helpful around the house. At the very least, keep your room clean and pick up after yourself.
- Always have your equipment well organized. Your parents should never have to nag you about getting ready for games and practices.
- Once you earn a driver's license, drive yourself to practices.
- If you're exhausted or sore from baseball, do something about it; don't whine to everyone or walk around in a bad mood. Take a nap if you're tired. To relieve sore muscles, try taking a bath with Epsom salts.
- The night before, look up directions or addresses to new baseball fields where you will be playing the next day.

JOIN THE CONVERSATION!

Organization, your academics, and your social life are all very important components to becoming a successful **COMPLETE ATHLETE**. Learn more by downloading the app today!

ACADEMICS

Throughout Levels 1 and 2, a youth baseball player should have been laying the foundation for strong **ACADEMIC** achievement. Level 3 is the time to develop plans for getting into college and earning scholarships.

WHERE TO FIND ANSWERS REGARDING COLLEGE ATHLETICS >>

The National Collegiate Athletic Association, or NCAA (www.ncaa.org), serves as the athletics governing body for more than 1,300 colleges, universities, conferences, and organizations. The organization has a wide range of resources available to help youth baseball players and their parents understand the eligibility requirements for earning scholarships and playing sports at the college level, including the following:

- *NCAA Guide for the College-Bound Student-Athlete*, which is available as a free download at www.ncaa.org
- The NCAA Eligibility Center's resource page at www.eligibilitycenter.org (click on "Resources")
- www.ncaa.org/student-athletes/future

UNDERSTANDING SCHOLARSHIPS AND ELIGIBILITY

Each NCAA Division has different scholarship opportunities and eligibility requirements. For example, only NCAA Divisions I and II colleges and universities award athletics scholarships. Division III colleges and universities do not award athletics scholarships, but they do provide academic scholarships as well as need-based financial aid.

ELIGIBILITY TO PLAY FOR A DIVISION I COLLEGE OR UNIVERSITY* >> According to the NCAA website, to be eligible to play at a Division I college or university, an athlete must complete the following:

COMPLETE 16 CORE COURSES >> Finishing at least 10 of these core courses before the seventh semester, with at least seven courses in English, math, or natural science.

EARN A GPA OF 2.3 OR HIGHER IN THE CORE COURSES >>

EARN AN SAT OR ACT SCORE MATCHING YOUR CORE-COURSE GPA ON THE DIVISION I SLIDING SCALE >>
The sliding scale balances your test score with your GPA. If you have a low test score, you need a higher GPA to be eligible. If you have a low GPA, you need a higher test score to be eligible.

REGISTER WITH THE NCAA ELIGIBILITY CENTER >>
Ensure you meet the NCAA amateurism standards and are academically prepared for college coursework. The NCAA Eligibility Center certifies the initial academic eligibility and amateur status of all college-bound student-athletes who wish to compete in NCAA Division I or II athletics.

ELIGIBILITY TO PLAY FOR A DIVISION II COLLEGE OR UNIVERSITY† >> According to the NCAA website (www.ncaa.org), to be eligible to play at a Division II college or university, a youth baseball player must complete the following:

---

*These eligibility guidelines are for students enrolling full-time at a Division I school after Aug. 1, 2016.
†These eligibility guidelines are for students enrolling full-time at a Division II school after Aug. 1, 2018.

COMPLETE 16 CORE COURSES » Finishing at least 10 of those core courses before the seventh semester, with at least seven courses in English, math, or natural science.

EARN A GPA OF 2.2 OR HIGHER IN THE CORE COURSES »

EARN AN SAT OR ACT SCORE MATCHING YOUR CORE-COURSE GPA ON THE DIVISION II SLIDING SCALE » The sliding scale balances your test score with your GPA. If you have a low test score, you need a higher GPA to be eligible. If you have a low GPA, you need a higher test score to be eligible.

REGISTER WITH THE NCAA ELIGIBILITY CENTER » So that you ensure you meet the NCAA amateurism standards and are academically prepared for college coursework. The NCAA Eligibility Center certifies the initial academic eligibility and amateur status of all college-bound student-athletes who wish to compete in NCAA Division I or II athletics.

ELIGIBILITY TO PLAY FOR A DIVISION III COLLEGE OR UNIVERSITY »

Although Division III schools do not offer athletics scholarships, 75 percent of Division III student-athletes receive some form of merit- or need-based financial aid. If you are planning to attend a Division III school, you do not need to register with the NCAA Eligibility Center. Division III schools set their own admissions standards. For more information about Division III schools, go to *www.ncaa. org/d3* or go visit websites of the schools you're most interested in attending.

IMPORTANT STRATEGIES »

- Spend time with your family researching colleges.
- Learn what your colleges or universities of choice look for in a student-athlete, and be realistic about your ability to succeed.
- Consult with your school counselor throughout high school to ensure you are on track to graduate having completed all required NCAA-approved core courses.
- Plan to take the PSAT during your sophomore year to get an idea of how you might do on the SAT.
- Plan to take the SAT and ACT a few times. The higher your score on these exams, the more scholarship money will be available to you at any NCAA college or university.
- Maintain your grades and graduate on time.
- Visit *www.eligibilitycenter.org* to learn more about opportunities available at NCAA colleges and universities.

BRENTON SULLIVAN » *Recruiting, like any talent search, is not a perfect science. You're trying to make sure that you're ready if an opportunity arises. That means you have to know about NCAA eligibility requirements and if you qualify. You need to make sure that you're eligible and able to maintain it when recruiters knock on your door. You also have to ask how you will pay for college. You have to know what you can afford and factor in any athletic and academic scholarship you may earn.*

PARENTS » If you have been fortunate enough to have a son who is being recruited by college coaches, remember this when deciding with whom you will sign your National Letter of Intent. Coaches often leave and scholarship money can change! Make your choice with this simple question in mind: Will your son be happy here for four years, whether his play (playing time) is good or bad?

Think about such important factors as affordability if scholarship changes, location, weather, academics, and athletic school spirit. I see too many parents making decisions based on a scholarship percentage offered from the baseball coach, all so they can stroke their own ego and say to other parents, "We were offered 90 percent."

A school may be a poor fit for many reasons. Truthfully, many parents think big college scholarships are like big signing bonuses in professional baseball: The higher the investment means more time to fail and be safe if the player doesn't have a great first year. This couldn't be further from the truth.

If a college has that much invested in your son and a limited amount of scholarship money to use each year, they will most likely ask you to lower your scholarship amount for the following season or leave. I see this every year. It's just one more reason to not dwell on percentage as your main reason for choosing a school.

COACH MIKE MARTIN >> *My best advice to high school athletes who want to play ball in college is to keep academics first. Don't put the sport first. These days, if you don't have the grades, you're not going to be able to go to the school you want to go to. It's that simple. Coaches want student-athletes with proven self-discipline in the classroom, knowing these individuals will not fall apart when they get to college. You can't slide in high school; you've got to bear down. If you fall behind early, all the tutoring in the world may not get you back on track for at least a semester. You may end up in summer school making up classes.*

No baseball player wants to do summer school as that means he can't play in a summer league. Do the best you can do in high school. That will make you much more interesting to coaches, and guys who can handle pressure in the classroom are better prepared for the pressure on the field.

SOCIAL LIFE & ROLE MODEL

At Level 3, a baseball player's **SOCIAL LIFE** may take a back seat to academics and sports. However, maintaining positive relationships with friends is still very important. Young people who maintain strong friendships tend to be happier and more successful in school and on the field.

At this point in a baseball player's life, his closest friends may be fellow baseball players because these are the people with whom he spends most of his time. These are also the people with whom he has the most in common. In fact, many lifelong friendships are formed between youth athletes who play the same sports. However, lifelong friendships are usually only developed by people who know how to recognize—and be—a true friend.

HOW TO RECOGNIZE—AND BE—A TRUE FRIEND >>

BE TRUSTWORTHY >> True friends earn trust by always having each other's back and never sharing anything said in confidence.

SHARE VALUES >> True friends share many of the same values, such as getting good grades or playing fair.

BE EMPATHETIC >> True friends are happy for each other when good things happen and sympathetic when bad things happen.

CONTINUE TO BE A GOOD ROLE MODEL >> Model good behavior by avoiding illegal drugs, alcohol, tobacco, performance-enhancing substances, and other risky behaviors.

AGREE TO DISAGREE » Friendships are tested when disagreements occur, but true friends work to move past the disagreements and don't abandon the friendship because of them.

Sometime friendships do end because of disagreements. For instance, say you have a friend who gets into drugs or alcohol or engages in other risky behaviors. He may try to get you to participate as well. Although you may want to try to help him, his problems are probably too big for you to handle. Your best bet may be to walk away from the friendship so that you can continue to be a good role model for your other friends.

LIVING YOUR SPORT

Levels 1 and 2 revolved around playing for the love of the game, practicing more, and studying the rules of baseball. At Level 3, a youth player who lives the sport of baseball begins to study professional players, especially those who play the positions he wants to play.

HOW TO STUDY PROFESSIONAL PLAYERS »

- Watch professional games, especially when your favorite athletes play.

- Closely watch players who play the position(s) you want to play.

- Read articles and any books about your favorite players.

- Put together a list of questions you'd like to ask if you ever get the opportunity to meet a professional baseball player who plays the position(s) you want to play.

ATHLETES >> At the gym, we encourage our athletes to "walk with lions" and find players with the same mission who have great practice habits. Younger athletes can learn a great deal by following and observing better athletes.

Daniel Robertson, a Major league infielder for the Tampa Rays, is someone I encourage other players to emulate. He stretches more and warms up longer than anyone else, sometimes taking more than 45 minutes before he starts his lifts, eye-hand coordination drills, or hitting in the cage. Daniel never skips an exercise, never passes up on his smaller arm-care drills, and never leaves out mobility work between his big lifts.

His attention to detail is incredibly advanced. After a workout, he goes to the back of the gym, throws a baseball against the wall, and tries to catch it, working on short hops, backhands, and forehands. He also throws a reaction ball, which has an uneven surface and bounces randomly, off the wall.

I have seen him do this for so long after lifts that I gave him a key so he could lock up or come in anytime he wanted. Now, other kids are doing the same thing, trying to emulate one of the top young big leaguers in baseball.

DANIEL ROBERTSON » *Bringing a reaction ball into my practices has helped considerably. Just throwing it against the wall gives me a real cardio workout as well as skill practice for reacting to tough hops in games. A reaction ball is a different animal from a baseball. You have to keep your feet moving since you don't know where it will go next. It's a great workout, too and I'm glad other players have started following suit.*

JOIN THE CONVERSATION!

Live your sport & join the **COMPLETE ATHLETE** community of athletes, parents, and coaches by downloading the app today!

TREVOR HOFFMAN

One of the best things my parents did for me was encourage me to be involved in whatever activities I wanted to pursue. I really can't emphasize enough how much I benefitted from not specializing young. My high school basketball coach, Tom Gregory, was someone who approached his job with enthusiasm for every aspect of the game.

This not only fostered appreciation for basketball in his teams but also the necessary components for all kinds of success. His coaching philosophy was to teach the person, not the athlete; in other words, he adjusted his strategy to the young men he had each year, focusing on our individual strengths, rather than trying to force every player to fit the same kind of mold.

As a result of being a 5'8" guard, I came to develop a new appreciation for how far sheer effort can take you. Even though I didn't have the traditional basketball player build, I found that playing defense didn't require me to have much athleticism; my success or failure instead hinged on my ability to think on my feet.

The challenge of pushing my body beyond the limits of endurance I thought I had, the thrill of competing against the clock, the rapid-fire pace of the game versus the much slower pace of baseball—these all made me appreciate the gains that I could make simply through hard work and a willingness to keep grinding.

The mental toughness that comes as a result of that is invaluable. I also got to enjoy a different kind of camaraderie as part of a basketball team. Baseball is a team sport played individually, but basketball taught me to be a less selfish player and to learn to work with my team in a whole new way. The skills and experiences I learned in basketball proved essential in shaping me as an all-around athlete and a better teammate, especially as I prepared for what I hoped would be a college career in baseball. Unfortunately, even though I was a very good high school baseball player, I did not have a solid sense of self-evaluation. By that I mean that I did not necessarily understand where my talent stacked up next to my peers beyond the handful of other communities in Southern California.

I had fantastic high school coaches, but because I was part of a strong team and my brothers' successes had paved the way a bit for me—Greg from his time as the JV coach and Glenn who was then in the pros—I had a bit of an inflated sense of my abilities. When I didn't get any scholarship offers to play baseball in college, it was a harsh splash of reality.

Even so, the hard work and tenacity that I had learned as a fairly small high school basketball player ended up being the key to my success (combined with outstanding coaching, of course), as it helped me develop as a junior college baseball player and, eventually, earn a scholarship to the University of Arizona.

My brothers also made a point to mentor me regarding the importance of staying committed to my education. I remember pulling up to a fast food restaurant with Greg after practice one day and noticing some men laying bricks outside. Greg looked at me very seriously and said, "There is a lot of pride in what those men are doing—

they are doing honest work for an honest paycheck, and that is worth your respect … but it is also very hard work. If you don't want to work with your back, you need to make sure you stay committed to your school."

The impact of that moment really stayed with me; I had the luxury of choosing what path I wanted for my life. If I wanted to go a different route than manual labor, I needed to take the necessary steps to make that possible.

That is an important lesson for young athletes to learn— and the earlier, the better. It's too easy for athletics to take precedent over schoolwork. In fact, some parents even encourage it, viewing it as an investment in the future when it's time for college scholarships or the MLB draft. But a scholarship is not guaranteed (as I can personally attest), and a professional career is not forever; your son needs to be prepared for a career and life outside of baseball. As my brother pointed out, there is pride in any kind of an honest profession, but as parents, you've got to make sure your son is equipped with the knowledge and skills he needs to have plenty of options for his future.

JOIN THE CONVERSATION!
See more from Trevor Hoffman and other pros in the **COMPLETE ATHLETE** app.

IN LEVEL 4

An athlete is among an elite group of athletes who have made it further than most. College athletes must learn how to handle themselves in the public eye, to manage many new demands and responsibilities, and to continue to maintain their nutrition and physical health in a new environment.

4.1 ATTITUDE

A positive **ATTITUDE** is essential to an athlete's success both on and off the playing field. A positive attitude is something that can be developed with practice, just like any other skill. A **COMPLETE ATHLETE** makes a habit of demonstrating the following five attributes:

RESPECT

SPORTSMANSHIP

TEAMWORK

PROFESSIONALISM

LEADERSHIP

RESPECT

At Level 4, a baseball player becomes a college-level student-athlete. By achieving Level 4, a student-athlete has consistently demonstrated **RESPECT** for his coaches and game officials, his teammates and opponents, and himself. These skills will likely be tested in college.

At college, a student-athlete is under a great deal of pressure to perform—both on the field as well as in the classroom. There is also greater temptation to engage in activities that do not contribute to his health and well-being, such as drinking alcohol or taking performance-enhancing drugs or other illegal substances. At Level 4, a student-athlete should always demonstrate respect for the game of baseball.

Taking performance-enhancing drugs violates the rules—as well as your integrity—and should be avoided at all times.

ATHLETES » Athletes who reach this level have been through a lot and have overcome many obstacles. Talent helps athletes reach this level, but things here are different from previous levels. Everyone who plays at this level has talent, but now other factors come into play.

We had an athlete who learned that talent wasn't enough at this level. He partied a little too much in high school but got away with it since he was more talented than everyone else. In his freshman year of college, he didn't change those habits. Despite that, he was talented enough to have a good year. But things got worse during his sophomore year.

He partied even more, thinking he could get away with it due to his talent. But he started to decline, his fastball slowing and his pitching worsening. He lost focus, stopped showing up early to practice, and cut down on weights. He ended up suspended after a failed drug test. After returning, he didn't change his habits and failed a second drug test. That one ended his time with that school—his dream school, by the way. He had to come to terms that his baseball career was over, and he had only himself to blame.

However, I wasn't going to let him give up because I knew how great a kid he was despite his demons and prior mistakes. So I reached out to him in the summer and asked him if he was ready to commit to doing things right and getting back on the field. He said he was, and I found him a new home at a smaller college near his former college. It wasn't a big D1, but it was a great baseball fit for him and he was able to have a second chance.

Thankfully, he cleaned up his act. He got his priorities in order and got rid of the bad habits. He was able to rededicate himself and turn things around. He even was able to go back and graduate from the school he originally attended after his senior season at his new school. He also ended up getting drafted that year and is doing amazingly well as a professional player. Even better, he's now talking to kids, telling them to avoid the pitfalls he fell into. It's very cool to see.

SPORTSMANSHIP

Good **SPORTSMANSHIP** starts with respect for one's teammates, opponents, coaches, and officials. It also includes maintaining a positive attitude when dealing with adversity—or victory.

At Level 4, the stakes are higher, and the pressure to win is greater. Student-athletes often play with a great deal of emotion, putting everything they've got into the game. Some find it difficult to contain their emotions before, during, and at the end of a game.

A Level 4 **COMPLETE ATHLETE** demonstrates good sportsmanship by practicing the following:

• Refraining from trash talking the other team or players, both online or before the game
• Graciously shaking hands with opponents before and after each game
• Winning without gloating
• Sincerely congratulating the other team, even if his own team loses

ATHLETES >> Every year in the College World Series, a few schools come out of nowhere. Some of them have never played a televised game all year, let alone a nationally televised one. There's a lot on the line for these programs, from building a national reputation to boosting recruiting. Sportsmanship is especially important, as largely unknown programs look to leave a good impression. Athletes at these small schools should be careful not to get too emotional by throwing helmets in the dugout or lashing out at umps after bad calls. Players who do that at this level will be on camera and leave a bad impression of themselves, their families, and their programs. That's why it's important to do things the right way and always show great sportsmanship, no matter at what school or level you are playing and no matter if there are 40 fans in the stands or 4 million watching on TV.

TEAMWORK

TEAMWORK means working together as a group in order to achieve a goal. In sports, players contribute their individual skills and efforts in cooperation with their teammates to win games. Learning to play as part of a team, and not just as an individual athlete, is important at every level of play.

A Level 4 youth baseball player has dedicated a great deal of his time and energy to get to this point, and he has a right to be proud of his accomplishment. So do his teammates.

At this stage, each member of the team has reached an elite level of play. Baseball is no longer just a game; your team might play for a championship at some point. Teammates need to commit to each other to the point of feeling like family, all working toward a common goal. It almost feels like an earlier level when team members learned to trust each other so that they could work together effectively. Team-building exercises should be taken very seriously, and any personality issues must be worked out immediately.

ATHLETES >> In college, freshmen come into a program in groups of four to nine new players. All of them are in the same boat, trying to find their way and become part of the team. However, because there are numerous NCAA rules that state when players can begin practicing with coaches, team-building doesn't start on the field. Instead, it starts in the weight room and around campus as players spend time together and get to know each other. Even though practices may not yet be in full swing, this is an important time for college players.

One of our athletes attended a major Division I school with another player from our area. This other player had a bad reputation. While talented, he was a problem, partying too much, always picking fights, and letting his ego get the best of him. During his senior year of high school, this bad attitude cost him a place in the draft, even though he was rated very high as a prospect on the field.

It predictably got even worse in college for this player, even though everyone still expected him to be an All-American as a freshman and get drafted by his junior year. But before the season even began, he was involved in two fights and was suspended. Two months after he arrived, the college released him and sent him home.

Later on, during winter break when college players come back home to train, I talked to one of his teammates, who happened to be the team captain. The captain called him an "idiot" and told how he picked a fight with his teammate at a college party the first week of school and acted as though he was the best player on the team even before the season had started. "You could see that the entire team quickly figured out this guy was not going to be a team guy, and he wasn't going to try to gel with the group at that early stage," he told me.

This story serves as a reminder that you are entering a new culture and need to be respectful before you insert yourself. Team bonding begins before the games start. If you work hard, put in extra time, and listen, you will fit right in. Then it becomes all about performance on the field. New players should get a vibe for the team and how the program works before they take the field. Athletes have to mold themselves within that team and its culture to be successful.

PROFESSIONALISM

As a baseball player becomes a student-athlete, **PROFESSIONALISM** takes on new meaning. He now plays for a college team, and he needs to represent that team with dignity and pride—on the field, off the field, and with his online presence. Not doing so can have serious consequences in terms of any scholarships he may have received.

A student-athlete should always maintain professionalism in terms of his appearance, his attitude, and his actions. Some examples include the following:

- Learning rules of etiquette and always displaying good manners
- Dressing appropriately off the field (no obscene T-shirts, tattered clothing, etc.)
- Wearing team apparel that represents his college or university, not another one
- Keeping his online and social media presence noncontroversial
- Staying away from inappropriate situations, such as parties where drugs may be present
- Avoiding the bar scene, especially if he is underage

ATHLETES >> College athletes should look the part. They are being scouted by pros, who are looking at what the athletes do on the field physically and watching what they do off or even around it. They observe how players handle themselves in the dugout, how they behave in the locker room, how they talk to their parents and other players, what they are posting and liking on social media, and how they react after a win or loss.

Cody Ponce, one of the top prospects for the Milwaukee Brewers, was one of our athletes who attended a Division II school. While he didn't get lots of attention out of high school and wasn't being groomed for the pros as they do now, he was ready. He always handled himself well and looked different from his teammates.

He showed confidence and strode to the mound between innings. He was always positive, saying hello to the umpire when he picked up the ball, acting like a pro. All mannerisms he was taught by his strong mom and dad who emphasized all these traits, and made sure he was always better off the field before on the field.

He reminded me of any major leaguer who has come down to the minors to hit or pitch some rehab innings. Everything just looks different with the major leaguer: the confident walk, the pristine uniform, top-of-the-line equipment, the leather belt instead of the cheap cloth ones handed out to every minor leaguer.

You can tell right away he is a big-leaguer. The true pros are more aware of the environment and are not making things about themselves. You rarely see them throw their gloves or toss things around when frustrated.

They talk to the coaches and other players between innings. Cody reminded me of a pro by the way he handled himself and took care of his uniform and equipment.

When I first noticed this, I was walking in from the parking lot trying to catch one of Cody's starts. The parking lot was a couple hundred yards from the field, and I was not sure if I was going to miss the first inning of his game.

As I looked toward the field, I saw Cody taking the mound. Right away, he looked like a big leaguer playing with college kids. That first impression before he even threw a pitch was powerful. Many scouts had been saying the same thing about him all year. Little things like this can go a long way toward affecting a team's final decision on drafting a player and can be the difference in a couple hundred thousand dollars in slot money.

Of course, not all college players present themselves as pros with their uniforms and actions. They look sloppy and dirty and handle situations poorly. The scouts pay attention to these behaviors. They notice all of it.

Another college team had its starting catcher go down with an injury during the playoffs. There were two options: a freshman with no experience or a senior who the coaches assumed was prepared and mentally ready to play even though he had been a backup most of his career. Because this was the playoffs, the game was being shown on local TV. The coaches turned to the safe bet in the senior. But he had an awful first at-bat, striking out on three pitches and looking unprepared—like a deer in headlights.

The senior handled this badly, stomping back to the dugout, throwing his batting gloves, cursing at the umpire because of a blown second strike call, and tossing his bat. To make things worse, he actually slipped on the dugout stairs and fell. The coach saw this and had had enough, yanking the senior from the game and putting in the freshman. The freshman was prepared and ended up having a good game, knocking in three runs on a bases-loaded double. He started the rest of the playoffs, while the senior had blown his chance by acting unprofessionally and calling attention to himself. He embarrassed himself and the entire program.

LEADERSHIP

A baseball player may have become a team **LEADER** in high school. As he moves on to college play, he may continue in that role. A leader for a college-level team must be able to do the following:

• Communicate effectively and present expectations clearly
• Listen patiently and open-mindedly to the input and opinions of others
• Treat all teammates fairly, never playing favorites
• Be open and honest with teammates

JOIN THE CONVERSATION!

Sportsmanship, leadership, and professionalism are all core aspects of becoming a **COMPLETE ATHLETE**. Learn more by downloading the app!

COACHES >> Injuries or surgeries can feel like a dead end to your career, giving you no hope of regaining your old healthy form. But truthfully, many athletes have overcome major injuries and come back, often stronger than they were before the injury. I have been on both sides of the coin when it comes to injuries, as a player and as a coach.

In 1999, I was plagued with a shoulder issue that wouldn't go away, and after multiple stints on the DL and MRIs, I was finally diagnosed with a torn labrum. It was such a frustrating time because I had been given MRIs that didn't show any structural issues, but finally after another attempt to come off the DL failed, the team decided to use a Gadolinium contrast (dye shot) to show more clearly if there was a tear. It lit up like a Christmas tree, and I went into surgery soon after.

I could have been upset that I wasted a year on and off the DL, but I decided to attack this like I did my career. That meant asking questions from players with similar injuries, listening to experts, and doing everything I could to come back stronger after surgery and rehab.

I worked harder than I ever did, doing more shoulder, core, and elbow exercises than ever before, which I believe many players who take their rehab seriously come back stronger than before surgery. By the time I was back pitching at full strength, less than a year post surgery, I was throwing higher velocities than before surgery.

As a player I learned how hard I had to work physically and mentally to regain my old form and get back on track. As a coach it allowed me to have a positive perspective to help a particular athlete who was given the devastating news that his ulna collateral ligament (TJ) had been torn.

I remember the phone call from him like it was yesterday. I was sitting down, about to take a bite out of my lunch, when his mom's number came up on my phone. I knew they had been to a doctor's appointment to look at his elbow. Unfortunately, I had a feeling it wasn't going to be good news—a few days earlier he had described the feeling and sound his elbow made in his last game.

What will never leave my memory is the sound of a young man crying uncontrollably, screaming into the phone that his career was over and that he will lose his D1 scholarship (he was already committed before injury).

I had never heard anyone in so much pain asking for my help. As a player who had been through that feeling, I told him the truth, that I believed he would come back from this injury and would also be stronger than he before. I told him I would be right there with him every step of the way. He was a strong kid with a great work ethic, and I told him that would help him bounce back faster than others who didn't know how to work.

And I would come to find out that his school would honor his scholarship even though he would be missing a year. His mom told me later that, when he received the news that he needed TJ surgery, he dropped to his knees in shock and began crying uncontrollably. Then, the first thing he asked while crying was for her to give him her phone, and he ran out of the doctor's office to call me.

A parent once told me you never know what kind of impact you are going to make as a coach. I truly know what that means, and it is why, as a coach, you have to show great character and presence among every athlete you meet, no matter how long or how short you are with them.

ATHLETES >> Our players head off to college after working hard. We cover tons of things with them on the physical, mental, and preparation sides. But things are far different in college. It's another level and much more challenging than what they have previously experienced. Athletes have much more independence in college, and they have to adapt to new situations: academics, time management, new coaches, and a new system.

Athletes must realize that once they reach college, coaches will be very different. They most likely won't be the smiling and charming recruiters with whom you spoke during your last couple years of high school. Now it's all about wins and losses. Coaches' styles may be harsher than you are used to, and they may not be who you thought they were. That's OK. It's time for you to forge you own your path and learn to adjust to different personalities. With the pressure to win at this level, coaches depend on players to do things on their own. That means players have to grow into better leaders.

One thing I encourage my athletes to do is to learn and emulate from their team leaders. I tell my athletes to watch the most successful players on the team. These players aren't always the most popular members of the team, and they may not be fun guys to hang out with. But college is more than just having fun and partying, especially for athletes who want to play professional baseball. These athletes should get to know the best players on the team and ask questions about what the coaches want to see. For instance, you can ask that leader, "What coaches like players to stay after or go early for extra work?" or "Who are the bad seeds on the team I need to avoid?" This helps athletes become more successful earlier on and creates good habits for the future.

PREPARATION

At the college level, **PREPARATION** takes on a whole new importance. It is more than just your personal discipline with practice, diet, rest, and mentality; it also involves watching game tape, studying your opponents, and being emotionally focused both on and off the field. Athletes who prepare for every game and practice naturally emerge as team leaders. These are the players who make the starting roster because they have a winning attitude that drives the way they hone their skills and prioritize their time and academics.

A **COMPLETE ATHLETE** prepares to perform on the field of play by continuously improving on the following:

PRACTICE

NUTRITION

HYDRATION

RECOVERY

MENTALITY

JOIN THE CONVERSATION!

Don't miss out on all the conversation happening in the **COMPLETE ATHLETE** app. Join today!

PRACTICE

At Level 4, an athlete is playing baseball at the college level, and **PRACTICE** sessions are supervised by an elite coaching staff. However, because they are working with an entire team of baseball players, staff members will be limited in terms of time they are able to spend with individual athletes.

Additionally, NCAA colleges and universities have rules in place to limit the amount of practice and conditioning time required and supervised by coaches.

• Student-athletes who want to achieve higher levels of success—or even just maintain the success they've already achieved—must practice drills and perform conditioning activities independently or alongside teammates without direct supervision.

HOW TO WORK INDEPENDENTLY OF COACHES »

• Develop your own practice schedule that includes the skills you want or need to improve as well as those you've already mastered.
• Create a conditioning/skill work schedule and routine that fills in gaps that you may be missing in your college program.
• Incorporate the technical knowledge you've gained up to this point.
• Listen to your body to train and practice safely with minimal risk of injury.
• Continue to practice and perform conditioning activities throughout the offseason to maintain your athleticism.
• If possible, continue to work with a private coach.

ATHLETES ▸▸ College players will have two breaks—winter and the far longer summer vacation—when they will be away from their coaches and programs. But that doesn't mean athletes have downtime, even as they go home and visit their friends and families.

Athletes need to stay in shape, work hard, and maintain their fitness. Chances are, especially during winter break, competition is right around the corner. Players need to find places to train, hit, and pitch. Summer and winter breaks are the busiest times of year for our gym. It's a good to see athletes who know how important it is to return from breaks stronger and fitter than they were before. Often, these are the times when coaches start making decisions about starters and redshirting players. Staying focused on improvement during breaks can give players the edge needed to make the squad or win a starting job.

There are different options over summer break. Some coaches send players to summer ball teams, which can be grueling. Some of our guys have come back from summer ball tired but also needing to get back in shape. Even though they play many games, these individuals don't have access to a lot of facilities and can quickly lose overall strength. Some of the athletes who make the biggest gains over the break are the ones who opt out of summer ball. Instead, they dedicate their summers to training hard in the gym, putting on weight, and working on technique.

Summer break doesn't mean a break in playing baseball. Cody Ponce, one of our athletes, used his summers to advance his career by training hard and returning to school in better shape than when he had left. Cody was not recruited heavily out of high school.

He ended up going to Cal Poly-Pomona, a Division II school. During his freshman and sophomore summers, he worked out a lot at the gym, put on size, and improved his strength. He ended up exceeding expectations as a pitcher, leading the league in saves. His velocity rose from the high 80s in high school to the mid to upper 90s in college.

During his junior year, he was invited to the Cape Cod League, where he had one of the best summer ball sessions and made the All-Star team. The Brewers drafted him in the second round. That wouldn't have been the case had he taken off his summers.

COACHES >> Many athletes starting to play college ball assume they are going to receive more instruction and time with coaches than they did in high school and earlier. The truth is that college coaches have a huge roster to work with. They also have recruiting duties and NCAA compliance eating up their schedules, limiting their hours to practice with individual players.

I tell my athletes when they leave for college to know what got them to this point. College coaches are just getting to know the players and might offer changes; some will work, while others won't. The more athletes know about themselves and what has gotten them to this level, the easier it is for them to determine if changes will help or hurt them.

We once had a college athlete, a good right-handed pitcher who was drafted but didn't sign. He was throwing 94 mph out of high school. He went to a big, successful school. He came back three months later during winter break, and his mechanics had started to change, making his pitches wild and decreasing his velocity.

When he came back in the summer, his velocity was down to 89 mph, a significant drop. Thankfully, we had video to help this player. Coaches, especially private coaches, should record their players on video. In the last session, coaches should talk on camera about everything they have worked on. That way, during downtime in the dorms or on the bus, players can watch the video, hear the voice that helped them get to this level, and make sure they employ the same techniques that helped them succeed. It's a far better reference point than solely relying on memory.

NUTRITION

As a youth baseball player becomes a college student-athlete, **NUTRITION** continues to play a key role in his life, not only for optimal performance on the field of play but also to obtain the vitamins and minerals he needs for optimal health.

LEVEL 4 ATHLETE NUTRITION GUIDELINES »

Each individual has different macronutrient needs, based on height, weight, age, activity level, and genetic background. The following macronutrient guidelines are based on age and estimated activity level for a Level 4 athlete:

- 45 percent carbohydrate
- 30 percent protein
- 25 percent fat
- No more than 7 percent saturated fat
- No trans fat
- 38 grams of fiber per day
- No more than 150 calories per day from sugar (37.5 grams or 9 teaspoons)

ATHLETES » Be sure to prepare yourself for the next level by knowing more about nutrition and how it can help you make those critical, consistent gains. Too often, athletes enter college not understanding how to eat and how nutrition can positively or negatively affect your performance.

Two of our athletes saw different results when they went to college. One of them went to a big school with a huge athletics program. The training table had a variety of food. The other athlete went to a smaller school where the athletics department did not have as many resources. Both of them left in the best shape of their lives and had worked out hard over the summer. When they came back after the fall semester, they looked very different. The one who went to the big school returned 25 pounds overweight. He simply wasn't the athlete he had been when he left.

Once he arrived at school, he ate more than he ever had before, taking in more calories than he was used to, and it showed. He should have taken advantage of the nutritionists many of these big schools have on staff. It can be very easy to gain "bad" weight either by eating too much junk, overeating, or even worse, falling into the trap of partying and drinking alcohol.

The other athlete came back much thinner and had lost a lot of muscle mass. The smaller school simply didn't have the funds to feed athletes the same as the larger college, and the meal plan did not help either. This athlete needed to be better prepared to live on his own and cook for himself. Not every school has a big enough budget to cover athletes' food. Athletes have to learn to adapt to this or their careers could suffer.

HYDRATION

Athletes should drink water before, during, and after practices and games. This is especially important on days when both temperatures and humidity levels are high.

HOW TO MAINTAIN PROPER HYDRATION* >>

- Before exercise, drink 16 to 20 full ounces within the two-hour period prior to exercise
- During exercise, drink 4 to 6 full ounces
- After exercise, replace 24 full ounces for every one pound of body weight lost during exercise

ATHLETES >> You can take many different approaches to your seasons and your offseason. One is to go about it status quo and do only what you are told to do by your high school coaches or other teammates. Or, you can take a more proactive approach and set goals of eating better, gaining strength, or resting your arm.

The latter obviously can give you the most bang for your buck, but can also come with some flak from people who may not have your best interest at heart or a big-picture approach to your individual development.

By that, I mean you may have to step away from normally scheduled activities, and this can be hard for old-school coaches to accept. Trust me, it will pay off for everyone in a big way. To try and get your skeptics to buy in, you will have to educate them, sharing the benefits and the reasons for your making this choice. You can find more than enough articles and information about the benefits of rest, nutrition, and strength training all over the Internet.

One of my athletes decided to really hit the nutrition and weight training hard after a frustrating sophomore year. He and his parents had a long, hard conversation to search out more beneficial ways to get improve over the summer and weighed the negatives and positives of stepping away from some high school activities to do more individual training.

His team and coaches didn't take the game as seriously as he did, and practices were unorganized and lifeless. He spent most of his time sitting around in the outfield shagging mindless hours of batting practice. When it was time for his bullpens each week, the coaching staff wasn't even watching or teaching. He saw this as an opportunity to get better leading into his junior year and decided to dedicate more time to training.

Four days a week he would lift, long toss, and work on his delivery. It wasn't easy, but that summer he started to see the gains. His body weight increased as did the velocity on his fastball, going from a low 80s pitcher with a lot of success to a upper 80s pitcher who couldn't be touched. Scouts were noticing as well and were asking what he was doing that had made such a difference from sophomore spring to end of that summer.

Even better, he kept training, and within a year, he had gained more than 20 pounds and a fastball that was reaching into the low 90s. This got the attention of college scouts quickly, and he committed to a major Pac-12 school and was drafted by an MLB team after his high school senior season.

Adapted from guidelines provided by the American College of Sports Medicine (ACSM)

The takeaway from this for athletes is to do more than you are asked to do. If all you are doing is what everyone else is doing, then you are only relying on your natural skills. But, if you were to take your natural ability and combine it with higher-level strength training, eating, and seeking out great instructors with years of success and experience, imagine how good you can become.

RECOVERY

Youth athletes need to eat and drink within 30 minutes of a practice or game to make up for calories they are burning and fluids they are using. Replenishing calories and fluids also aids in muscle **RECOVERY** and repair.

HOW TO REPLENISH CALORIES AND FLUIDS >>

- Drink 24 ounces of fluid for every pound of sweat lost within two hours of a game or practice.
- Consume 25 to 30 grams of protein plus an equal amount of carbohydrates within the 30-minute recovery window.

SLEEP >> Getting adequate sleep is difficult during this stage. Typically, college student-athletes "burn the candle on both ends." They're up early in the morning and late in the evening. According to the National Sleep Foundation, a Level 4 student-athlete should get 7 to 9 hours of sleep each night.

If you sleep six hours or less on a consistent basis, you may be setting yourself up for failure because your body cannot perform at an optimal level. Sleep deprivation can also affect hormone regulation, which makes your body crave more sugar and refined carbohydrates for quick energy. This is the opposite of what your body needs.

TIPS FOR GETTING MORE SLEEP AT COLLEGE* »

AVOID STIMULANTS » Such as coffee and energy drinks. If you must drink them, do so earlier in the day, and cut yourself off by noon.

WIND DOWN » Your body needs time to shift into sleep mode, so spend the last hour before bed in a calming activity such as reading. Avoid using an electronic device, such as a laptop, because the particular type of light emanating from the screens of these devices activates the brain.

---

*Adapted from the National Sleep Foundation

PRACTICE A RELAXING BEDTIME RITUAL >> A relaxing, routine activity right before bedtime conducted away from bright lights helps separate your sleep time from activities that can cause excitement, stress, or anxiety. All of these can make it more difficult to fall asleep, get quality sleep, or remain asleep.

ATHLETES >> Most college athletes will live in dorms, which usually mean having many people around them while they're trying to sleep. Even when athletes share a room, there can be problems, including different sports seasons and schedules for practices and games.

During the season, when baseball players need more sleep, football players and track athletes might be in party mode, making loud noises and keeping crazy hours. There are many distractions in the dorms that can cost baseball players valuable sleep.

One of our athletes looked awful when he came home. He blamed his roommate, who would stay up all hours playing loud video games. This made it tough for our athlete to sleep. I told him to get earplugs and an eye mask to help catch up on his sleep. He texted me back, letting me know how much of a difference the plugs and mask made. It was a simple solution and one that works for many athletes living in dorms.

MENTALITY

At Level 4, players focus on learning mental imagery. Mental imagery is simply seeing yourself perform successfully before you even step on the field of play. Student-athletes who can envision themselves performing successfully will perform better. Mental imagery takes practice and requires a great deal of concentration. However, the more your train your mind to focus on the right things, the more it will respond. You may even feel fatigued the first time you start to practice this.

Using all of your senses helps. For example, imagine the smell of the grass as you move along the field. See yourself getting ready to bat. Feel your foot as it moves into position, and hear the sound of the bat as it makes contact with the ball. You can also find apps that teach you how to train your brain to relax.

ATHLETES >> MENTALITY is the X factor for many athletes, giving them an edge. More and more, colleges across the country urge their athletes to use mental practice and mental preparation.

Tyler Witt, a very highly recruited left-handed pitcher who was one of our athletes, attended Wake Forest, where the coaches stressed mental preparation. His pitching coach would tell his athletes to go through an inning on the mound as if they were in an actual game. So Tyler, when his workout was over, would go up on the mound, take deep breaths, and visualize a game. He would visualize he was at Wake Forest's or a rival's stadium facing hitters. Tyler would go through pitch sequences, moving the ball in and out.

JOIN THE CONVERSATION!

Join us today for further tips, advice, and conversation by downloading the app!

He would go through his entire delivery, from the stretch to runners on base. It was great practice. Some guys would cut it short, but Tyler would visualize the whole inning and go through every step just as he would in an actual game, managing hitters, runners, and even the fans in the stands. Visualization has paid off for Tyler as he continues to grow as a pitcher.

Good friend and Vanderbilt University head coach Tim Corbin also shared with me that he has his players do the same thing between starts, but he actually takes it one step further and has them simulate everything down to a tee. Players have to be in full uniform, go through their pregame routine, stretch, pretend to throw, and even step off the mound to simulate deep breathing and refocusing during tough innings.

Training the brain to feel as though it has "been there, done that" in any situation is where the phrase "the game slowed down for me" comes from, a common phrase among elite players.

JON OLSEN >> *When playing in college, you learn very quickly that if you wear your emotions on your sleeve, pitchers can see that and will feed off it. Baseball is such a mental game. You have to learn to control your emotions; you have to practice that control just as you would any other skill. Some people are naturally unflappable or really good at hiding their feelings, but most athletes need to practice masking their emotions during a game.*

4.3 FITNESS

At Level 4, a baseball player is playing at the college level. He likely has a strength and conditioning coach who supervises **FITNESS** workouts. However, because that coach is working with an entire team of baseball players, he or she will be limited in terms of time spent with individual athletes. Additionally, at NCAA colleges and universities, rules are in place to limit the amount of practice and conditioning time required and supervised by coaches.

Student-athletes who want to achieve higher levels of fitness—or even just maintain their current level of fitness—must perform conditioning activities independently or alongside teammates without the direct supervision of coaches. This helps not only to establish a foundation of good fitness but also to teach good habits needed for success in higher levels of baseball.

LOWER-BODY STRENGTH

UPPER-BODY STRENGTH

FLEXIBILITY / MOBILITY

CORE STRENGTH

SPEED / QUICKNESS / ENDURANCE

LOWER-BODY STRENGTH

Level 4 builds on what you have accomplished at Level 3. You should be getting stronger, more explosive, and better balanced. You have seen that strength in the **LOWER-BODY** has been the difference in keeping you healthy and dynamic on the baseball field. At this level, you may be trying to make a college starting roster or just the traveling roster.

Chances are, your skills are at a very high level; now you must have elite-level strength in your lower-body to set yourself apart from the rest. We will push your test numbers higher because we know you are nearing the top of the baseball food chain, a place very few athletes reach. Most often, work ethic and strength are what separate top players from the rest. Now your times are extended, reps are higher, and distances have increased.

A great deal of power and torque for throwing and hitting comes from the hamstrings, quadriceps, and gluteal muscles. Exercises such as single-leg squats and jumps can help a baseball player develop the leg strength, posture, and mobility that lead to better baseball technique.

TO PERFORM SINGLE-LEG SQUATS »

- Stand on one leg while the other leg is lifted off the ground in front of the body. The hip should be bent to approximately 45 degrees and the knee bent to approximately 90 degrees.
- Hold out your arms straight in front of you, hands clasped together. From this position, squat down until the knee is bent to approximately 60 degrees.
- Return to the start position and repeat.

TO PERFORM A VERTICAL JUMP »

- Stand next to wall and reach as high as you can without lifting your toes or heel off the ground. Measure that distance from the ground.
- Stand away from the wall, jump as high as you can, and touch the wall.
- Measure the distance between standing reach height and jump height.

TO PERFORM A BROAD JUMP »

- Stand behind a line marked on the ground with feet slightly apart.
- Use a two-foot takeoff and landing, swinging the arms and bending the knees to provide forward drive.
- Jump as far as possible, landing on both feet without falling backward.

TO PERFORM A LATERAL JUMP »

- Stand on one leg with the foot at the starting line and hands on hips.
- Squat down quickly and then jump sideways as far as possible, landing on both feet without losing balance.
- Measure the distance jumped to the nearest foot.

UPPER-BODY STRENGTH

College coaches are looking at you to separate yourself from the competition, and the margin for error is small. Your **UPPER-BODY STRENGTH** may be the difference that allows you to drive that inside fastball out into the gap, throw out a speedster on the base paths, or recover after long, intense outings. College strength coaches will expect you to know what you are doing in the weight room before you even get to campus. If you have neglected that aspect, it will reflect poorly on you, setting you behind the returning class and incoming freshman competition.

At Level 4, tests are more difficult, times are extended, and distance is increased to push you and find out if you have been working to become a **COMPLETE ATHLETE** in the gym.

TO PERFORM A VERTICAL PULL-UP »

- Grasp an overhead bar using the neutral grip or underhand grip (palms facing toward body), arms fully extended and legs hanging straight down.
- Raise the body up until the chin clears the top of the bar.
- Lower again to the starting position, arms again fully extended.

TO PERFORM A SITTING MEDICINE BALL THROW »

- Sit on the floor with back against a wall and legs fully extended (about 2 feet apart).
- Hold a 5-pound medicine ball with hands on the side and slightly behind the center. Place back of ball against the center of the chest. Forearms should be parallel to the ground.

Rotational medicine ball throws follow the same motor pattern used in games. They help to teach youth baseball players how to transfer power from rotational movements such as swinging and throwing. It may be the single most important component in training to hit and throw harder.

TO PERFORM A ROTATIONAL MEDICINE BALL THROW

- Stand perpendicular to a start line (such as in a pitching or hitting stance).
- Hold a medicine ball in both hands, placing back hand on the back of the ball and the front hand under the ball.
- Draw the ball back with only a slight bend at the elbows, keeping the ball between the waist and chest.
- In one swift motion, fling the ball up and forward (optimally at a 45-degree angle).

FLEXIBILITY / MOBILITY

A good degree of **FLEXIBILITY** and **MOBILITY** leads to better baseball technique and helps to prevent injuries. As discussed in previous levels, the sit-and-reach test is used to assess and improve an athlete's level of lower-body flexibility and mobility. Likewise, the shoulder-stretch test is used to assess and improve an athlete's level of upper-body flexibility and mobility.

TO PERFORM THE SIT-AND-REACH TEST »

NOTE: You'll need a box that is 12 inches high, such as a milk crate. Tape a yardstick or ruler to the top so that the first 9 inches hang over the edge and the 9-inch mark is exactly on the edge against which you will place your feet.

- Place the box against a wall. Sit on the floor in front of the box with your legs straight in front of you and the soles of your feet flat against the front side of the box. (The overhanging part of the ruler should be pointed at your chest or midsection.) Keeping the legs straight and flat on the floor, stretch forward and reach along the ruler with one hand on top of the other, palms down.

- Stretch forward three times without bouncing; then reach as far as possible, holding at the farthest point for at least three seconds.

TO PERFORM THE SHOULDER-STRETCH TEST >>

- Stand with feet slightly apart.
- Place one hand behind the head and back over the shoulder with the palm touching your body and the fingers directed downward.
- Place the other arm behind your back, palm facing outward and fingers upward.
- Reach as far as possible, attempting to touch the fingers of each hand together.
- Repeat with the other side.

CORE STRENGTH

Now that you are in an exclusive group of athletic achievement, the room for error has decreased. Athletes with better balance and stability will have a huge advantage, and this is exactly what a strong **CORE STRENGTH** gives you.

As in Level 1, we have kept the plank, medicine ball throw, and hip-lift march to test lower back, glute, and hamstring strength.

In Level 4, we will continue to test a side plank to show any imbalances in the core from one side to the other. Imbalances can lead to injury and overworked muscles on one side. The plank and the side plank are great exercises for strengthening the core.

TO PERFORM A PLANK ››

- Get down on the floor with your hands apart slightly wider than shoulder-width, your arms straight and supporting your weight.
- Make sure your body stays straight. Your hips shouldn't be sticking way up in the air or sagging.
- Hold that position as long as you can.

TO PERFORM A SIDE PLANK ››

- Lie on your side with your legs straight.
- Prop your upper-body up on your elbow and forearm.
- Make sure your elbow is aligned with the shoulder.
- Brace your core by contracting your abs forcefully, and then raise your hips until your body forms a straight line from your ankles to your shoulders.
- Breathe deeply while holding this position.
- Repeat this exercise on your other side.

The hip-lift march helps to measure—and improve—the strength and endurance of the back muscles.

TO PERFORM A HIP-LIFT MARCH ››

- Lie flat on your back, knees bent 90 degrees and feet flat on the ground.
- Lift hips as high as possible; only shoulders and feet should touch the ground.
- Keeping hips at the same height, lift each knee in a controlled marching motion for as long as possible.

JOIN THE CONVERSATION!

Teamwork, respect, and community are all important parts of becoming a **COMPLETE ATHLETE**. Check out the app to learn more!

SPEED / QUICKNESS / ENDURANCE

As discussed in previous levels, there are two types of baseball speed:

Straightaway **SPEED**, on the base paths or in the outfield
Lateral, or side-to-side, **QUICKNESS**, such as when an infielder moves to get a ground ball.

The 30-yard sprint helps an athlete improve straightaway speed. The 5-10-5 Shuttle Run, or Pro Agility Drill, is a great way to improve lateral quickness because it helps to hone an athlete's ability to accelerate, decelerate, stop, and reaccelerate without losing balance. The Beep Test is a good way to measure and improve **ENDURANCE**.

TO PERFORM A 5-10-5 SHUTTLE RUN >>

- Set up three marker cones 5 yards apart.
- Start at the middle marker cone in a three-point stance.
- Turn and run 5 yards to the right side and touch the marker cone with the right hand.
- Turn around and run 10 yards to the left and touch the marker cone with the left hand.
- Finish by running back to the middle marker cone.

JOIN THE CONVERSATION!

Additional exercises, drills, and tips are available in the **COMPLETE ATHLETE** app today!

TO PERFORM A 30-YARD SPRINT >>

- Place two cones 30 yards apart.
- Starting at one cone, run as fast as you can to the other cone.

TO PERFORM A BEEP TEST >>

NOTE: You'll first need to download a Beep Test audio recording or Beep Test app, which will play beeps at set intervals. As the test proceeds, the interval between each successive beep reduces, forcing the athlete to increase his speed.

- Draw two lines 40 yards apart.
- Stand behind one of the lines, face the second line, and begin running when instructed by the recording.
- Continue running between the two lines, turning when signaled by the recorded beeps. After about one minute, a sound indicates an increase in speed, and the beeps will be closer together.
- The test is stopped when the athlete can no longer keep in sync with the recording.

LEVEL-4 FITNESS TEST

LOWER-BODY STRENGTH
- Eight full-range single-leg squats with each leg
- Vertical jump of 25 inches or greater
- Broad jump of 110 inches or greater
- Lateral jump of 90 inches or greater

UPPER-BODY STRENGTH
- 15 pull-ups for position players, 10 for pitchers
- 45 push-ups in 60 seconds for position players, 35 for pitchers
- Sitting medicine ball throw of at least 18 feet
- Rotational medicine ball throw of at least 50 feet with an 8-pound ball

FLEXIBILITY/MOBILITY
- At least 40 centimeters in the sit-and-reach test
- Shoulder- stretch test (pass or fail)

CORE STRENGTH
- 3-minute plank
- 0-second side plank on each side
- Hip-lift march with perfect form for 2.5 minutes
- Balance 45 seconds on each leg

SPEED/QUICKNESS/ENDURANCE
- 5-10-5 Shuttle Run in 4.8 seconds
- 30-yard sprint in 3.9 seconds for position players, 4.1 seconds for pitchers
- Beep Test minimum score of Level 10

TECHNIQUE

Level 4 is a very high level of baseball, requiring important shifts in the ability to perform or be outperformed during games. Remember, a **COMPLETE ATHLETE** not only masters the basic and advanced skills needed to play baseball but also understands the roles and responsibilities of every position on a team and how all the positions work together to win games. In moving to the collegiate level, you must use all the skills that you learned in Levels 1, 2, and 3 at even higher levels of efficiency, speed, and critical thinking to perform in a big game environment.

Most athletes at this level are in college and working toward making it to the minor leagues. Your college coach will be constantly testing and evaluating you to determine if you are doing what needs to be done to make the starting lineup. You will most likely be given only minimal time to show coaches you are ready for live games.

Intersquad games during the fall and winter may be the only chance you get to prove you can play. After you have proven that you have the ability to play at this level, can you continue to improve on your basic **TECHNIQUES** and learn new ones? You will still have tests to perform to measure where you are in your preparation; however, game assessment is what will ultimately get you to the next level of the game. Failure to produce at this level will result in loss of playing time or falling short of your dreams of becoming a pro.

THROWING

HITTING

INFIELD FIELDING

OUTFIELD FIELDING

GAME ASSESSMENT

THROWING

Good **THROWING** technique requires accuracy, arm strength, and proper mechanics to make plays. At Level 4, arm strength must be demonstrated at a high level. Throwing long toss and lifting weights are musts.

TECHNICAL TIPS >>

INFIELDERS Must demonstrate accuracy from any arm angle, anywhere on the field, and while on the move.

OUTFIELDERS Must be able to hit cutoffs and keep the ball in line with the target.

PITCHERS Must be able to throw first-pitch strikes with any pitch selection and throw strikes 65 percent of the time. Pitchers should also have the ability to throw strikes in any count, even with runners on base, and be quick to the plate. Walks will be the number one reason pitchers don't get chances to be in games, throw strikes!

CATCHERS Must throw accurately to any base, with a 1.95 or under pop time to second base.

HITTING

HITTING must be executed more frequently with greater strength in each swing, more contact, and fewer strikeouts. Athletes must also drive the ball to desired locations—right, center, or left field—depending on where the pitch was thrown.

You may be scouted by MLB teams who are grading you on multiple elements of your swings, bat speed, consistency, projected power, and average. All players at this level must be able to recognize pitch location and type of pitch when it leaves the pitcher's hand.

INFIELD FIELDING

Infielders must be able to anticipate where the ball will be hit. Your range around your position will be highly evaluated by your college coaches and scouts. Fielding most grounders should be routine at this level.

Remember, other athletes at this level will be able to take advantage of any errors in the infield, taking a base themselves or advancing a runner.

TECHNICAL TIPS >>

- Quick first step
- Good angles toward ball
- Receive ball cleanly
- Body control
- Quick exchange
- Anticipate where hitters hit certain pitches

COMMON MISTAKES >>

- Body out of position and hurried
- Too relaxed or nonchalant
- Inaccurate to first base

OUTFIELD FIELDING

OUTFIELDERS >>

- Must be able to anticipate the ball off the bat
- Quick first step, reaction
- Good angles
- Quick exchange
- Understanding of hitters' tendencies

COMMON MISTAKES >>

- Rushing glove exchange and getting timing off
- Missing cutoffs and poor throwing alignment

PITCHERS »

- Stay down on the ball.
- Be quick off the mound and cover a good amount of ground.
- Understand where you need to be after the ball is in play.

COMMON MISTAKES »

- Speeding up too much between pitches
- Poor footwork
- Not preparing enough before bullpen
- Not knowing where to be after the ball is in play

CATCHERS »

- Receive ball smoothly.
- Keep balls in the strike zone.
- Bring borderline pitches back in the strike zone.
- Block balls in the dirt, laterally, and in front of you.

CATCHERS COMMON MISTAKES »

- Missing bases
- Rushing
- Poor grip on ball
- Sloppy footwork

JOIN THE CONVERSATION!

For level-by-level tips & techniques, advice and conversation, please be sure to download the **COMPLETE ATHLETE** app today.

GAME ASSESSMENT

POSITION PLAYERS COMMON MISTAKES »

- Failure to execute drills from hitting tests
- Failure to make routine plays consistently
- Base running mistakes
- Taking bad at-bats into the field

PITCHERS COMMON MISTAKES »

- Showing emotions to coaches, yourself, or umpires
- Falling behind in counts in the game
- Lack of first-pitch strikes
- Poor command of off-speed pitches
- Poor control of running game

LIFESTYLE

A Level 4 baseball player has achieved a great feat: playing at the college level. Chances are, he has earned an athletic scholarship, an academic scholarship, or both. As a college-level student-athlete, he will need to employ all of the time-management and organization skills learned throughout this journey to maintain a satisfactory balance between sports, academics, family obligations, and social activities.

FAMILY

ACADEMICS

SOCIAL LIFE

ROLE MODEL

LIVING YOUR SPORT

FAMILY

A baseball player who has achieved Level 4 **COMPLETE ATHLETE** status has already laid the foundation for a lifelong positive relationship with his **FAMILY**. While at college, he should strive to maintain those positive relationships:

KEEP IN TOUCH » Set aside a specific day and time each week to talk to your family by phone. You can also communicate regularly via e-mail or text messaging.

STAY IN THE LOOP >> Even though you're living elsewhere, you'll want to feel connected with your family. Make sure your family keeps you informed of and included in important family decisions, activities, and updates.

VISIT FACE-TO-FACE >> Discuss with your family options for spending time together face-to-face during holidays, birthdays, or other special events. Skype and FaceTime when you can. Be actively involved in the planning so you can work around important sports and/or academic responsibilities.

ACADEMICS

Many student-athletes assume they'll go on to play their sport professionally after college—or even before graduating. The truth? There are more than 460,000 NCAA student-athletes, and less than 2 percent will go pro in their sports. The experience of college athletics and the life lessons student-athletes learn along the way will help them as they pursue a career in any field.

Student-athletes should take advantage of every resource and opportunity available to them at their college or university. In fact, many NCAA colleges and universities provide special resources to their student-athletes, including these listed below:

ACADEMIC TUTORS for both group and individualized tutoring.

ACADEMIC CENTERS offering tutoring space, individual and group study spaces, computer labs, and more.

INDIVIDUALIZED ACADEMIC COUNSELING to help student-athletes develop a plan for successfully managing their academic pursuits and reaching their academic goals.

CAREER DEVELOPMENT RESOURCES including career placement services for summer internships and job opportunities, resume workshops, alumni networking, email updates for job fairs, and internship postings.

Whether or not a student-athlete intends to pursue baseball at the professional level, he should absolutely maintain his grades throughout college and graduate with a degree in a marketable field. After all, even a professional sports career will not last forever, and a college graduate will have more opportunities available than one who has not earned a degree.

JON OLSEN >> *College is tough; it's a big transition. You have classes and baseball, and you have to find a balance because the expectations are higher in every aspect of your life. As a student, you have to maintain a full course load along with reading, homework, lab times, and papers. But as an athlete, you still make time for two hours of weights in the morning, four hours of practice in the afternoon, and games, of course. And you don't have your parents there to make sure you keep it all straight.*

Everyone comes in the same: You're all great players with a lot of talent and potential. But it ultimately comes down to how each person handles the change from high school. Some guys can't handle the pressure but some really thrive off those high expectations. The more prepared you are, the better you'll do.

COACH MIKE MARTIN >> *It's fun to see student athletes come in here as boys and leave as men. There are exceptions, of course. I mean, you have the Buster Posey types who come into the program with their heads on straight; they're already so mature and just keep growing from there. These are the guys who really stand out; they are the ones a coach really wants to see—the ones they know have come to get a degree.*

Buster gave a figure that it would take to sign him out of high school; the offers didn't meet it. Instead, he came to Florida State and became an Academic All-American and the Scholastic Player of the Year. He was going to be a first-round draft choice his last year, and what did he do? He stayed and pulled a 3.85 GPA his last semester at FSU.

That's what I like to brag about. These are people who have their ducks in a row. And he's not the only one. B.J. Stewart, James Ramsey, several other guys—they focused on their academics in college and ended up being top draft choices too. These are the kinds of players a coach wants on his team. The guys who show up to get an education and play ball while they are at it are the ones who are going to ultimately have the most success.

SOCIAL LIFE & ROLE MODEL

At Level 3, baseball players learned how to recognize and value a true friend and be a good **ROLE MODEL**. These attributes are also important at Level 4. With all the pressures on student-athletes, strong friendships are vital to their emotional health. True friends will listen and sympathize when that's needed, and they will provide fun and companionship when that's needed.

Once again, it's important to be considerate of friends' time and commitments and responsible when it comes to one's own. Nonetheless, carving out time for friends is an important part of a balanced lifestyle.

When it comes to socializing at college, temptations to behave badly are everywhere, and consequences can be dire. There are parties where alcohol may be served. Illegal drugs and other substances are often readily available on college campuses. Stressed-out friends may engage in impulsive, dangerous behavior and insist that you join them.

Student-athletes can be kicked off the team and lose their scholarships for many reasons. Their best bet is to continue to be a good role model by avoiding social situations that can lead to trouble.

COACH MIKE MARTIN >> *Leaders are not born. They are made by their parents. They are made by the people with whom they associate. They are made by their attitude, desire, and being a solid individual who cares about everybody on their team. This is true from the earliest levels of play.*

Buster Posey didn't eat with his teammates when we were on the road. He ate with the managers. He ate with the equipment guys. I'd never had a player do that.

JOIN THE CONVERSATION!

Not sure about where to apply to college? Get more information in the **COMPLETE ATHLETE** app!

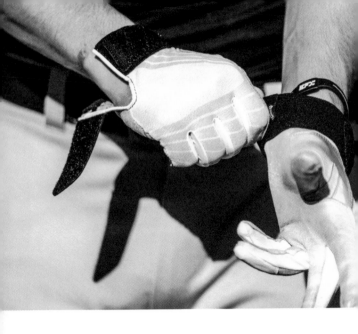

You know why the Giants are winning every year?
Because Buster is over there, and everybody loves Buster.
When he got hurt, he didn't feel sorry for himself; he
busted his butt, got back, and won another ring for his
team. He came from a family that taught that kind of
respect and hard work.

We have another player on our team named Drew
Mendoza who also had parents who stressed a good
attitude. Drew broke his jaw in practice when a pitch
caught him in the mouth.

It was a serious injury, and he couldn't talk for a long time.
When he came into the locker room a few weeks later,
while he was still healing, someone asked if he had
anything to say.

He went to the chalkboard and, with a huge smile, wrote, "Thanks, John!" (That was the guy who threw the pitch.) It was such a lighthearted, funny moment, and it made everyone crack up. I could see that Drew was going to be a future leader of FSU baseball because of how well he handled that situation and how positive he remained throughout. His attitude had such a positive effect and upbeat influence on the other guys.

One more example: Recently, I was at a wedding of one of our top players and when I looked up to the front of the church, I couldn't believe it. This guy who was our bullpen catcher was the best man. It wasn't one of our top players who went on the road to every game, but a guy who was there as a workhorse in practice. Why? Because he had had such a positive attitude for four years that all his teammates loved and respected him.

That young man never complained that he wasn't out front; he was happy doing what he was doing. It turns out that he was one of the most popular players on the team even though he never played. His mom was sitting right beside me during the ceremony, and she was every bit as positive and encouraging. After that wedding, I let it be known that we weren't traveling without him from there on out. He is living proof that you don't have to be the best player on the team to be a leader.

LIVING YOUR SPORT

At Level 3, youth players who live the sport of baseball begin studying professional players, especially those that play the positions they want to play. This activity will continue at Level 4 as the student-athlete becomes an even more diligent student of the game and an enthusiastic fan. One professional recruiter told the story of a student-athlete who, when asked about his favorite player, talked about a lesser-known player in glowing terms. The recruiter immediately recognized someone who was a true student of the game.

MLB PITCHER >> *When I was in high school, I was "the guy" on my team and one of "the guys" in the league. But in college, it was a whole different ballgame. I was an 18-year-old facing 22-year-olds. The game was faster. The other players were stronger. The other guys were better. To be competitive, I had to work harder in the gym. I learned you couldn't solely rely on your skills. The same thing happened as I moved from college to the minors. I had worked my way up to become one of the better guys on my college team and was drafted. But everybody in the minors, at one point, was like me. They were the better guys on their high school and college teams.*

At every level you achieve, mistakes become more magnified. The higher you go, a missed pitch results in a batter hitting it harder than before. Of course, the same holds true in the majors. Most guys were the best players on their high school and college teams. They were also the better guys on their teams in the minors. You have to concentrate on little things. Everyone else at this level is a good player. What separates you are consistency and the ability to do the little things on a daily basis.

TREVOR HOFFMAN

When I did not get a scholarship to a four-year school out of high school, I was crushed—but I also wasn't ready to give up on my dream. What I needed was an honest self-evaluation of not only my skills but also the reality of my potential limitations.

I was a talented, but not exceptional, high school infielder who tipped the scales at 140 pounds and stood five feet, eight inches. In other words, no matter my ambitions, I had to admit that I was not necessarily at the top of any recruiter's list. However, I did have an offer to play baseball at Cypress Junior College, and I was hungry enough to take whatever opportunity was available to me. My time at Cypress ended up being one of the best things ever to happen to me and to my athletic prospects.

Cypress Head Coach Scott Pickler and Assistant Coach Bill Pinkham proved to be some of the most influential and inspiring leaders I would ever encounter in my baseball career. Coach Pickler was one of those exceptional communicators who just inherently understands how to reach people where they are and how to connect with players to draw the most out of them. He had such a deep understanding of the game and a truly great baseball mind; his enthusiasm for every aspect of practice was something that impressed me.

I had a good arm and had pitched a bit in Little League, so the coaching staff at Cypress was willing to let me try pitching when I expressed an interest. I threw eight or nine pitches to my teammates and coaches ... and then couldn't wait to get off the mound.

My self-evaluation was still a little inflated, but that experience was enough to help me realize that, for the moment anyway, I should focus on becoming the best middle-infielder I could be.

This helped remind me of how much I enjoyed the drudgery of practice, as strange as that may sound. Rather than viewing the mechanics and repetition of training as something annoying or to be gotten through to get to the good parts of baseball, I began to look at the hard work as a challenge, as an enjoyable sort of obstacle course on the way to becoming a better player.

What this meant for me was that I came to love the game not for the thrill it gave me when I won, but for the deep complexities of it and the strategy and sweat of every minute part of the training process. The game isn't just what happens during nine innings under the lights—it is the countless exhaustive hours spent slogging it out behind the scenes.

My brother Glenn once offered me some advice that has stayed with me. He was enjoying some success as a professional player, but he told me he saw guys who lost out on the chance to be called up or to make some other kind of major step forward in their career all because they weren't prepared.

They wanted it, they dreamed of it, but they had not put in the work to get ready and to stay ready for the moment that opportunity finally presented itself. I never wanted that to be me, so I learned to truly love the work rather than just the thrill of winning. "Never leave yourself with the question of 'What if … ?" Glenn told me. That became a kind of personal mantra.

After two years at Cypress, I was offered a scholarship to the University of Arizona and I entered that program more humble, but also more confident, and far more mature than I had been immediately following high school graduation. I was able to continue growing at Arizona thanks to a tremendous coaching staff and a support structure designed with a goal of student development. I had the resources to help me maintain the proper balance between school and athletics, and I found that my enthusiasm for the less fun parts of practice was beginning to pay dividends. We had a conditioning coach who had competed on the Czechoslovakian Women's Olympic lifting team, and her expertise really helped me get more aggressive with the weights program I had started at Cypress. As I started to see results, my self-esteem began to grow.

This was before conditioning was emphasized as a part of high school programs the way it is now, and as someone who had always been a "little guy," it was incredibly exciting not only to see my body begin to bulk up but also to feel my strength increase as I explored this new avenue for training. Something I learned to appreciate very quickly was the importance of the basics. Coach Jerry Kindall had everyone throw the ball so that he could see our grip because he didn't want to take for granted that all his players automatically knew the most effective way to fire it to the bases. He had reasonable rules and enforced them fairly, like the rule against his players using smokeless tobacco in study hall. He knew that it was bad for our health, even though it was so popular among major leaguers at the time.

When I tested that rule, I lost the opportunity to play in a game and had to watch it from a clump of trees by left field. Coach Kindall cared about the whole person. He showed his emotions, but he never lost control: I never heard the man use a single curse word, even when he was furious. I wanted to bring that same level of excitement and investment to every moment on the field and to every moment in training.

One of the most important benefits that the baseball program at Arizona provided, however, was the sense of fraternity and belonging that I found with my team. It can be intimidating for a kid to go from high school with a relatively small group of students to a college campus anywhere from 10 to 100 times (or more) larger than they are used to. Parents need to remember that, no matter how brave their son seems as he prepares to leave home for the first time and no matter how eager he is for the adventure, things are going to be scary at times. The best reassurance you, as parents, can have in his ability to adapt is going to be in how well you prepared him with a solid foundation of character and good sense and in knowing that he has a good group of young men and coaches with whom he can surround himself. I was very grateful for the leadership both on and off the field that I had during my time as a Wildcat because it enabled me to focus on what I needed to do to grow into the best possible person I could.

The path to playing in college may not always take the route we hope it will, but it is important that we use every experience as a chance to grow and mature as people and as players. I can't imagine that I would have been prepared for success later in my career without having the resources and coaching I had at Arizona, and I would not have been as prepared to get the most out of my time at Arizona without the time I first spent at Cypress Junior College. In other words, view setbacks as detours rather than roadblocks, and enter into those unforeseen experiences with an open mind and a willingness to make the most of these alternative opportunities.

IN LEVEL 5

A baseball player has reached the highest level of his career: he is now a professional. There are different tiers of professional baseball, however, ranging from summer leagues to Majors. In order to continue on the journey towards this ultimate goal, an athlete will need to make the very best decisions on and off the field —in everything, from nutrition to social media. Level 5 is the time to show off the foundational character skills learned since Level 1, and to be a real role model!

5.1 ATTITUDE

A positive **ATTITUDE** is essential to any athlete's success both on and off the playing field. A Level 5 **COMPLETE ATHLETE** makes a habit of demonstrating the following five attributes:

RESPECT

SPORTSMANSHIP

TEAMWORK

PROFESSIONALISM

LEADERSHIP

RESPECT

As a Level 5 **COMPLETE ATHLETE**, you must continue to demonstrate **RESPECT** for your coaches and game officials, your teammates and opponents, and yourself. As a professional baseball player, you should also demonstrate respect for the fans who come to see you and your team play. If someone asks for your autograph, be gracious and friendly. Remember, without the fans, you might not have a team to play on.

ATHLETES >> Professional athletes can choose different ways to portray themselves in a respectful fashion even as media glare intensifies. Fans grow far more interested in what makes athletes at this level so special, what makes them tick, and tips they can give to help others reach the same level.

If you are a Level 5 athlete, looked up to because of your on-field success, it is critical to avoid giving the impression that you are above everyone and unapproachable. Some bad seeds will always exist, however, and they can ruin many a fan's experience by appearing too busy for conversation or even a quick question. There will always be times when you may not want to be bothered, but in the gym or on the field, you should be open to using this time to help other players or coaches. Picture yourself in the shoes of a young athlete striving to reach your level. Imagine a MLB player giving you a few pointers or simply asking about your last game. These are conversations that are remembered for a lifetime.

An MLB Pitcher who trains with me in the offseason presents himself very well. It's amazing to see him engage with everyone. People who have only known him 3 minutes feel as though they have known him 30 years. He has no problem sharing information and tips with other athletes. He also talks about politics, movies, and everything else in the world. He has a great attitude, which makes him extremely engaging. He's helpful, offering tips when he sees someone with a bad throwing habit or ideas on how to improve a workout.

I have another athlete in our gym who acts the opposite. He is a good guy, but he doesn't want to talk with anyone. He comes into the gym grumpy with his head down and headphones on all the time. He makes the wrong impression, and many of the younger athletes at the gym say they cannot stand him even though they have never met him. They say things like, "He thinks he's better than the rest of the players here, acting as if he's in the major leagues when he's only in Low A ball." If people come to that conclusion after observing him for only a few minutes, what do the front office and big sponsors think? His negative impressions could have negative implications for future earnings and endorsements. No doubt, this athlete needs to be more respectful to everyone.

We see both kinds of personalities at the gym, but thankfully, more of the athletes at this level fit in with the MLB Pitcher's mold. A lot of the athletes coming through our facility have been here a long time. They have been able to adopt a lot of good habits when it comes to respecting themselves and know many people observe how they act and what they do.

SPORTSMANSHIP

Good **SPORTSMANSHIP** starts with respect for one's teammates, opponents, coaches, and officials. A Level 5 **COMPLETE ATHLETE** demonstrates good sportsmanship by the following:

• Playing by the rules and never cheating
• Acknowledging and encouraging his teammates
• Accepting responsibility for his mistakes
• Refraining from arguing with officials
• Winning and losing with grace

As a professional baseball player, you must always remember that you are not the only player on the team. Even if you're a star player, you can't win a game all by yourself. Demonstrate good sportsmanship by giving credit to your teammates and your coaches when you win a game. You should also acknowledge that the other team was a formidable opponent.

ATHLETES >> At this level, athletes' reactions to adversity are important in determining how they are portrayed. This is the case even in minor league baseball. Remember, media attention grows as players move up the ranks.

Of course, in the major leagues, the spotlight is ramped up even further, with major networks and many reporters covering players. Social media also becomes more important at this level, and athletes have to be very careful with what they choose to post and share. Everything the player does will be covered, especially if an athlete displays bad sportsmanship such as throwing helmets or bats, getting into fights, or taunting and insulting the crowd.

When I was on the Phillies, I had a teammate who played a bad game. As he was walking off the field, his emotions got the best of him. He flipped off the crowd and threw his glove in the stands. While my teammate thought he had worked the frustration out of his system and was done with it, his problems were actually just beginning. With his actions, he unleashed a media firestorm, which embarrassed him and the entire organization. There have been far worse incidents over the years. The pressure of being on TV, to win crucial games, to make the playoffs, and to get contracts can manifest itself in ugly ways. This makes sportsmanship even more important at this level.

NOTE >> What you post on the Internet never disappears, no matter how quickly you erase it!

TEAMWORK

A baseball player who reaches the professional ranks will likely join a team that is already a tight knit family. He needs to earn the trust of his new teammates and maintain that trust using the skills he has learned along the way.

ATHLETES » At this level, it's hard to put a finger on why some teams have good chemistry but others don't. Most of the teams with good chemistry have one or two players who are the heart of the team, full of energy. I call them connectors. A good example of this is Stephen Vogt, the Oakland A's catcher. He does all the little things in the clubhouse and keeps his teammates loose with his jokes and impressions. Guys like him are the reason why the A's continue to be such a great team even though they are in a small market with a low payroll. Players like Stephen Vogt are the quiet locker room MVPs, even though they may have teammates with better stats who serve as the "face" of the organization. But inside the clubhouse, there are always one or two guys who keep the team loose when things are going bad and keep things fun when they are going well.

A great example of a player who unified his team and kept things loose in the clubhouse is my good friend and former teammate Dan Pleasac. Dan came to the Phillies when I was only a rookie. Despite playing 20 years in the majors, Dan's youthful attitude was refreshing to have in our clubhouse, especially during a season full of turmoil and tension with our manager, Larry Bowa. Dan was always energetic and positive, which even rubbed off on the typically serious and angry Bowa.

One way Dan kept us loose still gets a ton of attention. Dan and I were sitting in the bullpen and talking about how funny it would be if he pretended to sucker punch me during a play in the game when the camera was panning over us. One of the reasons Dan and I get along great is because I'm as crazy as he is and enjoy keeping the game fun. That being the case, of course I said, "Let's do it!"

We planned it out and waited for the right moment. While in San Diego, we had the perfect chance when Bobby Abreu came close enough to the bullpen to catch a third out. As the ball approached, I took my position, pretending I was looking up at the ball but actually keeping my eyes down while waiting for Bobby to catch it. As soon as he made the catch, I said to Dan, "Now!" and he threw a "haymaker" at me. Unbeknownst to us, it was captured by local TV and is still talked about today (search on Youtube for "Dan Plesac punch"). These kinds of moments are immeasurable. They greatly help teammates to bond and unite with one another.

PROFESSIONALISM

As a Level 5 **COMPLETE ATHLETE,** a baseball player simply needs to be the professional that he is being paid to be by representing his team and his sport admirably. In addition to the list of do's and do not's presented in the previous chapter, a professional athlete must learn how to speak to the media correctly and in a way that presents his team in a good light.

ATHLETES >> During my time with the Phillies, everyone in the clubhouse had a lot of respect for Scott Rolen, our third baseman. Scott was an outstanding guy. He was the epitome of **PROFESSIONALISM**, winning respect on the field with his seven All-Star appearances and eight Golden Gloves. Scott also earned respect off of the field with his positive attitude. He is a **COMPLETE ATHLETE**, no doubt about it.

We had a stretch when we weren't doing well. We held a players-only meeting to deal with too many anonymous quotes getting out of the clubhouse, stuff about players not liking the coaches and management. During the meeting, Scott stepped up. He wasn't a vocal guy, but on the field, nobody spoke louder with his work ethic. Because of that, we all listened to what Scott had to say. "Listen, I'm going to be the guy who handles these interviews," he said. "Good or bad, I'm going to be the one handling and taking all the bullets."

It was cool to hear our biggest player say he would take all the questions. For the rest of the season, after games, the media would go directly to Scott. He would answer their questions very professionally, good or bad, on highs or lows.

Even if he had a bad game, Scott never ducked out of talking with the media. When some other players had bad games, they would hide in the training room and not come out for an hour, which usually worked since the media had deadlines to meet. Scott never did that. He would always go to his locker and wait for the media. He would wait for all the reporters to gather and then say, "OK, go ahead and ask questions." When it came to the media, like everything else, Scott was a pro's pro.

LEADERSHIP

Whether or not a student-athlete advances to the professional level, the **LEADERSHIP** skills he has developed over the years will continue to benefit him after he leaves college.

In corporate America, as on a baseball team, a strong, confident leader can inspire team members to accomplish goals that they can't accomplish on their own. This is one of the many reasons why numerous companies hire former athletes.

A former player may consider coaching, moving up from introductory levels to higher levels of coaching. According to the U.S. Bureau of Labor Statistics, employment of coaches is expected to increase much faster than the average for all occupations through 2022. Nonetheless, there will be a lot of competition for college and professional coaching jobs.

The athlete who has developed strong leadership skills will be a much more attractive candidate because he already possesses the following:

- Excellent communication skills that allow him to effectively teach and convey information to his team.
- The ability to make quick decisions, especially during games and other high-pressure situations.
- Effective interpersonal skills that allow him to relate to his players.
- Negotiation skills that allow him to solve problems in the best interest of everyone involved.

JOIN THE CONVERSATION!

Get more preparation tips in the **COMPLETE ATHLETE** app!

5.2 PREPARATION

PREPARATION refers to off-the-field activities, such as practicing skills, eating right, staying hydrated, getting enough rest, and mentally preparing for a game or practice. A **COMPLETE ATHLETE** prepares to perform on the field of play by continuously improving on the following:

PRACTICE

NUTRITION

HYDRATION

RECOVERY

MENTALITY

DANIEL ROBERTSON >> *Discipline is a huge part of being a professional baseball player, especially if you're living on your own. Unlike high school, you don't have your parents or someone else to whip you into shape. You have to take care of your body and be careful with what you are putting in it. You have to make sure you're eating right and sleeping well.*

PRACTICE

If you have become a Level 5 **COMPLETE ATHLETE,** you may already be playing baseball professionally. Just like Level 4, practice sessions will be supervised by an elite coaching staff. Nonetheless, a professional baseball player takes full responsibility for training and practicing safely, both independently as well as with the team. He knows his body well enough to know how to push himself while minimizing the risk of injury. After all, an injured player can't play at his full potential.

A Level 5 **COMPLETE ATHLETE** continues to **PRACTICE** the skills he has already mastered, including the basics. In addition, he develops and practices new and innovative skills that can provide a competitive advantage for his team.

ATHLETES >> At this level, athletes are the best in the game and always looking for an edge to make them better players with improved skills. One offseason, we decided to add a twist to the workouts of Daniel Robertson, a top prospect for the Tampa Bay Rays. I brought in Ziad Khoury, a well-known soccer coach, to help Daniel. At first, he looked at me funny when we talked about kicking a soccer ball against the wall and doing drills that soccer coaches do.

But, to his credit, Daniel was all in and jumped into it. After that first workout with Ziad, Daniel wanted to keep the drills part of his routine for the rest of the offseason. Being able to throw in a different sport, as long as it's safe, is an excellent way to get athletes to expand their workouts and make everything fresh if their bodies have adapted to current routines. Daniel enjoyed the new challenges. I think he's going to keep that mentality for a really long time.

DANIEL ROBERTSON » *I knew Ziad Khoury was one of the best soccer coaches in the country. Working with someone so knowledgeable could only help my preparation. Focusing on footwork with Ziad helped me develop a quicker first step, giving me better acceleration. It was a great opportunity—even if it meant longer days in the gym.*

NUTRITION

As a college student-athlete moves on to professional sports, **NUTRITION** continues to play a key role, not only for optimal performance on the field of play but also for optimal health throughout his life.

LEVEL-5 ATHLETE NUTRITION GUIDELINES »

Each individual has different macronutrient needs, based on height, weight, age, activity level, and genetic background. The following macronutrient guidelines are based on age and estimated activity level for a Level-5 athlete:

• 45 percent carbohydrate
• 35 percent protein

- 20 percent fat
- No more than 7 percent saturated fat
- No trans fat
- 38 to 40 grams of fiber per day
- No more than 150 calories per day from sugar
  (37.5 grams or 9 teaspoons)

ATHLETES >> As pitching prospect Cody Ponce prepared for his first spring training with the Brewers, I urged him to make a good first impression and show up to camp in the best shape of his life. During spring training, staff is observing how good and determining how serious of an athlete they are. Cody stands 6'6" and is around 250 pounds, but we urged him to come to camp in better shape than last season to show the Brewers that he was serious and willing to sacrifice to play well for the team.

Cody worked hard in the gym in the offseason, but his biggest breakthrough came in the kitchen, where he focused on nutrition and changed his diet. This helped him lose weight and he looked great. The Brewers' brass noticed and even posted about it on their website. By showing up to spring training in better shape, Cody prepared for success over a long season. He took nutrition seriously and it paid off.

HYDRATION

All athletes should drink water before, during, and after practices and games.*

- Before exercise, drink 16 to 20 full ounces within the two-hour period prior to exercise.
- During exercise, drink 4 to 6 full ounces.
- After exercise, replace 24 full ounces for every one pound of body weight lost during exercise.

ATHLETES >> Back in 2000, when I was playing with the Philadelphia Phillies, we played the New York Yankees on one of the hottest days of the year. On summer days, Veterans Stadium felt as though it was boiling. It was up in the 90s with heavy humidity, but it was around 140 degrees on the turf that day.

I knew it would be a tough game; the Yankees had won the last two World Series and would win it again that season. I made sure to get lots of water in me the night before the game, and during the pregame warmup, I made sure to stay hydrated. That's important, especially for a player like me who sweats a lot.

Adapted from guidelines provided by the American College of Sports Medicine (ACSM)

While I pitched well that game, what I really remember about it was the heat. The cameras were zooming in on my hat because the front of it was dripping as the sweat came down like it was almost raining. That's how wet my entire hat was. My jersey was also soaked.

I threw a pitch and heard a fluttering sound. I thought a moth had flown by me right when I pitched the ball. When I got the ball back from the catcher, I looked around for a moth before I threw the next pitch and I didn't see anything. I threw a fastball and, sure enough, heard the sound again.

I finally figured out the noise was coming from my shirt. It was so wet that, when I moved my arm fast to throw the pitch, it made a noise that sounded like a shirt being held outside the window of a moving car. Despite the strange noise, I adjusted.

After the game, I had an interview. The media asked if I had noticed many of the players changing uniforms because of the heat and sweat and wondered why I didn't do that. They asked if I was superstitious. I replied with a straight face, "No, no, it's bad luck to be superstitious." That quote ended up on the cover of USA Today.

As a side note, the day before I had known it was going to be a tough day with the heat because my teammates had lined up extra pairs of shoes and an ice bucket. During the game, they iced the bottoms of their shoes before putting them on and switched them out every three innings. That's how hot the turf was that day. I had never seen that before. Regardless, the players who excel when it's that hot are the ones who stay hydrated.

RECOVERY

A Level 5 athlete needs to eat and drink within 30 minutes of a practice or game to make up for calories they are burning and fluids they are using. Replenishing calories and fluids also aids in muscle **RECOVERY** and repair.

HOW TO REPLENISH CALORIES AND FLUIDS »

- Drink 24 ounces of fluid for every pound of sweat lost within a two-hour period of a game or practice.
- Consume 30 to 35 grams of protein plus an equal amount of carbohydrates within the 30-minute recovery window.

SLEEP »

Sleep is still very important for muscle recovery and repair at this stage. Inadequate sleep will have a negative effect on athletic performance, and your body will not be able to "bounce back" as easily as it did when you were younger. According to the National Sleep Foundation, a Level 5 athlete should get 7 to 9 hours of sleep each night.

Obviously, research cannot pinpoint the exact amount of sleep needed by a particular individual, which is why it's so important to pay attention to your own individual need for rest and recovery. One way to do this is by assessing how you feel on different amounts of sleep.

- Are you productive, healthy, and happy on seven hours of sleep? Or do you need closer to nine hours of quality sleep time to feel this way?
- Do you wake feeling groggy, or do you bounce out of bed ready to take on the day?

- Do you depend on caffeine to get you through the day?
- Do you feel sleepy when driving?

TIP >> Experimenting with different amounts of sleep time can give you a better idea of your particular needs.

ATHLETES >> Most professional baseball players don't get to the major leagues. Riding a bus for 8 to 12 hours, as some minor league players have to do, is different from staying at the Ritz Carlton and flying on charter planes. When players have long road trips, they have to get some rest, especially if they are starting the next game.

There are plenty of variables that can impact your rest, making it difficult to get some sleep. When players are on a road trip, they should bring a backpack and fill it up with more than just food and drinks. Some of these buses show movies until 3 in the morning, depending on when the last game ended. I encourage players to bring sleep aids such as earplugs or very good earphones that block out noise. Players also need to bring pillows and blankets on these trips. Most players remember to bring a pillow, but they don't often think about packing blankets.

These buses can get cold, but it's usually warmer toward the front. The back of the bus is usually louder since that's where guys play cards or make noise. I always recommend that whoever is pitching the next day sit in the front or middle of the bus. It's also important for players to rest in their hotel rooms once they are off the bus.

JOIN THE CONVERSATION!

Recovery, sleep, and nutrition are all important for your health and best performance on the field. For tips & techniques from coaches and professionals, please download the **COMPLETE ATHLETE** app!

MENTALITY

At Level 5, focus remains an important part of mental preparedness. More and more elite athletes and sports programs are incorporating mindfulness, meditation, and other practices into their training regimen.

According to Dr. Kristen Race, Ph.D., an expert on brain-based mindfulness solutions, "Mindfulness helps train the prefrontal cortex, the part of the brain that creates a calm and alert state of mind, which helps us stay focused, avoid distraction, and perform at our best."

Practicing mindfulness is not easy, but like everything else in sports, the more you do it, the easier it becomes. Dr. Race suggests the following tips for practicing mindfulness:

ENGAGE IN MINDFUL BREATHING >> Every morning as well as before a game or practice to create a calm and clear state of mind. Sit comfortably, close your eyes, and start to deepen your breath. Inhale fully and exhale completely. Focus on your breath entering and exiting your body. Start with five minutes and build up from there.

CONDUCT A BODY SCAN >> This can release tension, quiet the mind, and bring awareness to your body in a systematic way. Lie down on your back, palms facing up and legs relaxed. Close your eyes. Start with your toes and notice how they feel. Are they tense? Are they warm or cold? Focus your attention here for a few breaths before moving on to the sole of your foot.

Repeat the process as you travel from your foot to your ankle, calf, knee, and thigh. Bring your attention to your other foot and repeat the process. Continue to move up to your hips, lower back, stomach, chest, shoulders, arms, hands, neck, and head—maintaining your focus on each body part and any sensations there. Breathe into any areas that are holding stress and try to release it.

JOIN THE CONVERSATION!
Follow your favorite pros in the **COMPLETE ATHLETE** app!

PAY ATTENTION TO YOUR INTERNAL DIALOGUE » which can reflect—or even shape—your mental state. Instead of thinking, *"I hope I don't strike out,"* speak in terms of what you want to achieve, for example, *"I'm going to get on base today."*

ATHLETES » Level 5 athletes are on the same physical level, so separation between them is going to be small. This makes mental preparation even more important at this level.

When I played for the Phillies, Curt Schilling, one of the most clutch players ever, took detailed notes on almost everything in the game. Before the game, he would fill up his notepad as he watched tapes and studied hitters

Besides taking notes on other players, Curt would focus on the umpires. He had a good feel for who was umpiring the game, who would be behind home plate, and each ump's strike zone. If Curt thought an umpire routinely gave away more fastballs away for strikes, he would take advantage of that. It was a unique way of preparing for the game.

DANIEL ROBERTSON » *There's a big mentality change when you become a professional baseball player. It comes down to how you prepare and how consistent you are over the long haul. Most high school teams play 30 games, but plenty of minor league teams play more than 140. Teams in the majors play 162.*

Of course, players at this level have more skill and power. But it really comes down to mentality and how badly you want to win over the course of a long season.

 FITNESS

Level 5 is the highest level of baseball. At this level, your own dedication to **FITNESS** will make you not only stronger than your opponents but also more flexible, faster, explosive, and healthier.

All of the exercises and tests below have been described in earlier sections. Your goal is to compete against your previous scores and always strive to improve.

LOWER-BODY STRENGTH

UPPER-BODY STRENGTH

CORE STRENGTH

LOWER-BODY STRENGTH

As a Level 5 professional, you are at the top of your game physically; you are stronger, more explosive, healthier, and more balanced than ever. You are staying fit during crucial practices, getting more playing time because of it, and seeing the difference on the field.

Keeping your fitness and health during practice and games may be the difference in being called up, earning a higher salary, or being chosen to play for an All-Star team. Stronger legs have made you faster on the base path and field. If you are a pitcher, you can maintain your velocity and sharpness of your pitches. Single-leg squats are easier, your balance is top-notch, and your jumping is exceptionally high. Congrats, you are ready for Level 5 testing and dominating any challenge!

TO PERFORM A TRIPLE BROAD JUMP >>

- Stand behind a line marked on the ground, feet shoulder-width apart.
- Use a two-foot takeoff and landing, swinging the arms and knees to provide forward drive.
- Jump as far as possible three times in a row, landing on both feet without falling backward.

NOTE >> Stretch out approximately 30 feet of rope or use a tape measure to mark jump direction and aid in recording jump distance.

UPPER-BODY STRENGTH

You may now be playing against players 5 to 10 years older than you. You may be just as skilled, but are you just as strong? Managers, scouts, and coaches will be looking to separate you from the competition, so the margin for error is minuscule. At this level, decisions may come down to matchups with other teams just as skilled; therefore, skill may not be what is most important at some positions. You don't want to be on the bench due to your lack of strength!

CORE STRENGTH

You are in the best shape of your life, playing against some of the most elite players in the world. Every athlete is out to either beat you or take your job—so staying healthy can be as important as scoring a run, hitting .300, or keeping your ERA below 3.00.

This is where a strong core is crucial for a baseball player. You need your hips to be strong to deliver accurate, crisp throws, and your lower back needs to be able to support all the torque that comes with moving quickly to catch a pop fly. A weakness in your core simply means you are likely going to be injured sooner rather than later.

JOIN THE CONVERSATION!

Fitness is key to performance. Get more tips and how-to's in the **COMPLETE ATHLETE** app.

LEVEL-5 FITNESS TEST

LOWER-BODY STRENGTH
- 10 full-range single-leg squats with each leg
- Vertical jump of 28 inches or greater
- Triple broad jump of 45 feet or greater
- Lateral jump of 95 inches or greater

UPPER-BODY STRENGTH
- 18 pull-ups for position players, 12 for pitchers
- 50 push-ups in 60 seconds for position players, 40 for pitchers
- Sitting medicine ball throw of at least 20 feet
- Rotational medicine ball throw of at least 60 feet with an 8-pound ball

FLEXIBILITY/MOBILITY
- At least 45 centimeters in the sit-and-reach test
- Shoulder-stretch test (pass or fail)

CORE STRENGTH
- 3-minute plank
- 60-second side plank on each side
- Hip-lift march with perfect form for 3 minutes
- Balance 60 seconds on each leg

SPEED/QUICKNESS/ENDURANCE
- 5-10-5 Shuttle Run in 4.5 seconds
- 30-yard sprint in 3.6 seconds for position players, 3.9 for pitchers
- Beep Test minimum score of Level 12

 TECHNIQUE

At this highest level of technical ability, you will be required to perform on the highest stage. Playing professionally will consist of many challenges and sacrifices. Now, you are constantly under the microscope—under pressure to perform on the biggest stage—and it is one that few get to experience. Remember, as a **COMPLETE ATHLETE,** you are responsible for continuing to master the four previous levels to play well at Level 5. Understanding the tactical roles and responsibilities of players, which can change within systems, will test your technical ability to the highest level.

Playing at the professional level is the greatest honor in the game of baseball. Mastering these technical tools and performing consistently in this environment is the final challenge on your journey to being a **COMPLETE ATHLETE.**

At this level, you will be graded and monitored extremely close by your team or even by other teams' scouts. Taking your skills for granted can be a huge mistake and lead to erosion of the talents that got this far. Constantly working on your basic skills while developing new ones is crucial to stay at this level for many years. Scouts will use a grading scale to evaluate you. (Check MLB Grade Scale on Page 293.)

THROWING

HITTING

INFIELD FIELDING

GAME ASSESSMENT

THROWING

At Level 5, greater arm strength must be demonstrated. **THROWING** long toss and lifting weights are musts to stay healthier and stronger than your competitors.

INFIELDERS must demonstrate accuracy from any arm angle, from any place on the field, and while on the move.

OUTFIELDERS must be able to hit cutoffs and keep the ball on line with the target.

PITCHERS must be able to throw first-pitch strikes with all pitches, throw strikes in any count, and throw strikes at least 65 percent of the time. Pitchers also should also have the ability to throw strikes with runners on base and be quick to the plate.

CATCHERS must be accurate throwing to any base and have a pop time of 1.95 or under to second base.

HITTING

HITTING must be executed more frequently with greater strength in each swing. Athletes must also drive the ball to desired locations—right, center, or left field— depending on where the pitch was thrown. You must mastering pitch selection, knowing your strengths within the strike zone. Depending on your position, you may need to show above-average power as well. Pitchers will search out and find your weaknesses if you don't adjust and work daily on your hitting skills.

INFIELD FIELDING

Infielders need to be error free and able to make difficult plays that require great range. You must be able to anticipate where ball will be hit based on the type of pitch or hitter. Fielding most grounders should be routine at this level. Remember, other athletes at this level will be smarter and faster, so errors can lead to big innings and, eventually, loss of playing time and the end of your career.

TECHNICAL TIPS >>

- Take quick first step
- Know hitters' tendencies
- Position yourself with good angles toward ball
- Receive ball cleanly
- Know pitch locations and selections and how that affects your position
- Make quick exchange

COMMON MISTAKES »

• Rushing glove exchange and getting timing off
• Missing cutoffs and alignment of throw

PITCHERS »

• Stay down on ball.
• Be quick off the mound and cover a good amount
  of ground
• Understand where you need to be after ball is in play

COMMON MISTAKES »

• Falling behind in the count
• Speeding up too much between pitches
• Lack of preparation

CATCHERS »

• Receive ball smoothly.
• Keep balls in the strike zone.
• Bring borderline pitches back inside the strike zone
• Block balls in the dirt, laterally, and in front of you

COMMON MISTAKES »

• Missing bases
• Rushing
• Poor grip on ball
• Sloppy footwork

GAME ASSESSMENT

POSITION PLAYERS COMMON MISTAKES »

- Failure to execute drills from hitting tests
- Failure to make routine plays consistently
- Base-running mistakes

PITCHERS COMMON MISTAKES »

- Showing emotions to coaches or umpires
- Falling behind in the count
- Lack of first-pitch strikes
- Poor command of off-speed pitches
- Poor control of running game

MLB SCOUTS GRADING SCALE »

The MLB scale is based on a 20 to 80 scale. A score of 65 or above implies particular individual may be a future MLB star.

- 20 to 30 Well below-average MLB player
- 40 Below-average MLB player
- 50 Average MLB player
- 60 Above-average MLB player

MLB GRADING SCALE

OBJECTIVE TOOL GRADES »

	Tool Is Called	Fastball Velo	Batting Avg	Homers	Rhh To 1B	Lhh To 1B	60 Yd Run
80	80	97	.320	40+	4.00	3.90	6.3
75		96	.310	35-40	4.05	3.95	6.4
70	Plus Plus	95	.300	30-35	4.10	4.00	6.5
65		94	.290	27-30	4.15	4.05	6.6
60	Plus	93	.280	23-27	4.20	4.10	6.7
55	Above Avg	92	.270	19-22	4.25	4.15	6.8
50	Avg	90-91	.260	15-18	4.30	4.20	6.9-7.0
45	Below Avg	89	.250	12-15	4.35	4.25	7.1
40		88	.240	8-12	4.40	4.30	7.2
35		87	.230	5-8	4.45	4.35	7.3
30		86	.220	3-5	4.50	4.40	7.4

5.5 LIFESTYLE

For student-athletes who become one of the rare few who move on to the professional level, life can sometimes feel like an open book. More people are watching them play, and they are in the public eye more than ever before. A Level 5 **COMPLETE ATHLETE** is one who continues to successfully balance all elements in his life:

FAMILY

ACADEMICS

SOCIAL LIFE

ROLE MODEL

LIVING YOUR SPORT

FAMILY

As a professional athlete, you should continue striving to maintain positive relationships with your **FAMILY** members by practicing the following:

- Setting aside a specific day and time each week to talk to your family by phone.
- Communicating regularly via e-mail or text messaging.
- Attending special family events whenever possible.
- Reassuring your family that they are still an important part of your life.
- Remembering that you're in the public eye and striving to make your family proud.

ATHLETES >> This game can make you feel pretty low as much as it can make you feel high. I remember a very pivotal period in my life that completely changed my attitude and perspective on how I live, how I react, what I view as success, and what a good day means. It happened in the span of a couple days back when I was pitching in the big leagues for the Phillies, during a time that everyone's lives changed.

I was starting a big FOX Saturday Game of the Week versus our NL East rivals, the NY Mets. I knew it was going to be a game carried all across the county and watched by millions of fans and a lot of family. But this was nothing new and I loved pitching big games. I felt so good going into the game. I had had plenty of rest, trained hard during the week, and had a great bullpen leading up to the game. But that was the only thing that went well, and I proceeded to have the worst game of my life. No matter what I did, I couldn't fix it. In fact, it was so bad that, by the time they took me out of the game without recording a single out, I had given up four runs, walked three, and given up three hits. I was booed off the field by a sellout crowd at my home field.

I have always been extremely hard on myself, but this was the lowest I had ever felt. I remember going straight past my locker and into the sauna near the showers. I cranked it up as hot as it could go and sat in there for an hour in full uniform. My jersey was soaked through. I felt as if the more torture I put myself through the faster I could get rid of the feeling of letting down my team and myself. It did nothing of the sort. The game finally ended, and I had to stand in front of 20 or so TV cameras and reporters and answer questions. That was miserable, of course, and I wished to be anywhere but there. Shoot, I would have rather been sitting in a dentist chair getting a root canal at that moment.

The next few days I carried that bad game into everything I did and walked around defeated. I wanted to be left alone in the outfield during BP and avoided talking to anyone. I was really taking it too hard and having a self-pity party. I even took it home, refusing to return calls and staying inside. We eventually took off to play Atlanta, and I knew I had one chance to make up for my previous game in my start against the Braves. But that game would be delayed and my life and attitude forever changed.

I woke up early to a phone call in our Atlanta hotel telling me to turn on the TV. Right then the second plane crashed into the Twin Towers in New York on September 11, 2001. After a few days of watching these world-changing events, it hit me like a giant slap in the face how selfish I had been to take my bad game so hard and to react so poorly when so many people were suffering over truly difficult situations. I was acting as though one bad game was the end of the world, and I was affecting others in my life unfairly. From that point on, I have aimed to face adversity or challenges as lessons to learn and show my athletes and families that, with the right attitude, "this too shall pass." As long as we stay calm, we can figure out a way to prevail and be better because of it.

MLB PITCHER » *At the start of my time in the minor leagues, the love of the game kept me going. But that can only take a player so far. After bouncing around the minors for a few years, there came a point when money became a major concern. Most minor league players don't make that much, yet expenses continue to mount. My wife and I were expecting our first child, and I had been thinking about getting out because I could not support them. It's impossible to support a family on the average minor league salary.*

While I felt as though I was good enough to get to the majors, after five years in AA, I was ready to call it quits and either go back to school or get another job. My wife convinced me to continue pursuing my dream, reminding me of how much work I had put in to achieve it. Later that year, I developed the knuckleball, which propelled me to the majors. That wouldn't have happened had my wife and I not talked things over.

ACADEMICS

As a Level 5 **COMPLETE ATHLETE,** you should have earned your college degree or be working toward that goal. As a professional athlete, you should take advantage of continuing education opportunities. Some sports organizations even provide signing bonuses that include money solely for school. Even if you're not provided education money, you should strive to expand your mind in new and different ways.

For example, business classes can help you later in life when you retire from sports. Taking classes just for fun, such as a foreign language class or an art class, can provide an opportunity to develop creative skills. Yoga classes can help you reduce stress and may even improve your performance on the field.

SOCIAL LIFE

You should continue to maintain a supportive **SOCIAL LIFE**. Make time for your friends when you can, and always strive to be a true friend. At the same time, be careful with whom you associate because you will be judged by the company you keep.

ROLE MODEL

These days, everyone has a cell phone with a camera. For a professional athlete—or anyone in the public eye—one mistake can be broadcasted internationally in a matter of moments. Remember, young people are looking up to you. Be a model citizen by behaving well and engaging in charity work and community service.

MLB PITCHER » *The biggest thing is to treat everyone the way you want to be treated. This kind of attitude has helped me weather the bad times. I've had a lot of ups and downs. I had some ups early on, but in the middle of my career, I had some doubts if getting to the majors was really going to happen.*

Then the knuckle ball came along. This attitude goes beyond baseball. It helps me throughout my life. I want to be a positive influence on everyone, especially with my fellow baseball players. I keep that in mind when I run into other guys in the locker room. I was in those guys' shoes at one point.

I want to be an open book and share what I've learned. I've been blessed throughout my life with plenty of guys who were open books to me. I want to be that for other people. I want to make sure that I'm approachable. I want people to come and talk to me without feeling intimidated.

If a guy has a question or just wants to talk, I want him to know he can approach me. While baseball is my job, it doesn't define me. It's not my personality.

LIVING YOUR SPORT

Then add this underneath: A Level 5 baseball player should **LIVE THEIR SPORT** by being active in the offseason when back home. Be a part of local little leagues or teams and help pass on the knowledge you have learned from being an elite level baseball player.

By showing your enthusiasm and passion for the game of baseball to younger generations, you can change the lives of many young baseball players. Teach them how you love to watch games or read books and articles on baseball, teach them how to live their sport.

JOIN THE CONVERSATION!

Study the techniques of the pros in the **COMPLETE ATHLETE** app!

TREVOR HOFFMAN

When a ballplayer reaches the pros, he may still have a foot in Level 4, depending on whether or not he is playing ball in a summer league somewhere. But once he has entered the draft and been brought into a team's farm system, he will very likely still face a number of challenges before he reaches a level where he feels as though he has "made it."

After college, I was drafted in 1989 in the 11th round by the Reds and was lucky enough to start my career with their team in Billings, Montana. It was such a beautiful, friendly city and a fantastic place for me to begin that stage of my career. But I will never forget one game when a man in the crowd had clearly had a bad day and decided to take out his frustration on me. In those smaller parks, it's amazing how loud single voices can be, and it proved nearly impossible to tune him out. In college games, people might trash-talk a bit, but it rarely escalates into the realm of full-on heckling and abuse. That game was a bit of an eye-opener for me in terms of realizing that being in the pros brings with it a whole new set of expectations. You are not automatically a hero just because you play for a certain team.

I moved on to other teams, but things weren't taking quite the trajectory I had hoped. My arm was good, but my hitting wasn't great. I was playing shortstop and third base, which was pretty much how I had always viewed myself as a player, but I was not putting up the kinds of numbers I should have been. That was when my manager, Jim Lett, approached me about trying my hand at pitching.

I have been blessed to have had great people in my life at major junctions in my career, people who saw potential in me and were willing to help me grow. Jim was one of those people. I'm lucky the Reds didn't just discard me, and I guess Jim recognized that I was someone who loved coming to the yard and would be willing to put in the work to develop a new, highly specialized skill.

He gave me room to experiment, and Mike Griffin, the pitching coach, was incredibly patient in helping me develop my arm. By 1991, I was pitching. It was a risk for the Reds' system and required an adjustment from me, but it paid off, and I will be forever grateful for that opportunity to reinvent myself in the middle of my career.

Unfortunately for those of us in the farm system, the Reds were doing exceptionally well at that time, even playing in the World Series in 1990, which meant that almost no one was getting called up from the minors. I found out that I had been drafted by Florida in the expansion draft while I was out to dinner with my dad. We were at a Shakey's Pizza when I saw the news announced on TV. I looked at Dad and said, "I guess I'm a Marlin now."

That's one of the things that a lot of kids don't realize about Level 5: You think when you're a professional that you will have control over your life, but the reality is that teams work deals and you may suddenly find yourself in a new city in the blink of an eye. You have to stay flexible and be willing to adapt if you want to make a life in this sport, whether embracing a new role on your team or embracing an entirely new team. I am glad I was able to share that moment with my dad. No matter how old you get, you still want to have your family around during major moments and periods of change.

I was traded to the Padres in 1993. Ironically, the fact that they were having a rebuilding season turned out to be really good news for me because it gave me a chance to learn and to fail without worry. I was a pitcher now, and I found that being a closer fit my personality beautifully. Closers need to be ready to go for every game and at any time, which meant that my affinity for the drudgery of practice and warmups was right at home. I might need to be ready after just a few innings, or I might not get in at all that night and would need to come back the next day to do it all over again.

It was fun to meet players and coaches who had also worked with Glenn, and his reminder about staying prepared so that I would never miss an opportunity still echoed in my ears. I never wanted to waste a chance to learn from the people around me, so when I noticed that one of my teammates, Danny Elliott, had a change-up grip I could copy, I knew I needed to work on developing that for myself.

I had a good fastball, but I knew a change-up would allow me to come back from an injury sooner. It ultimately gave my career an extra boost of longevity because I did end up with several injuries that might have been career-ending if I did not have a way to play around them.

All of this fed into a kind of mental toughness that is essential to remain a Level 5 player. You have to transition from one demand to another without getting ruffled, all while keeping your focus on the task at hand. The biggest challenge is learning to focus on the moment—not the expectations or possible outcomes—and just keeping it simple to get the job done.

It can be hard to silence the voice in the back of your head that knows it isn't easy to walk into the clubhouse when your pitching has blown the lead your teammates worked to gain.

It's equally tough to keep from celebrating prematurely that you were able to secure a win from what they created. It is those individual moments of laser focus to meet the immediate demands right in front of you, and for which you have spent months or even years preparing, that allow you to appreciate everything that comes after and to make something great out of the big picture.

That's true for baseball as well as life.

APPENDIX 1:
AN OVERVIEW OF BASEBALL

GENERAL RETURN TO THROWING PLAN
by Dave Coggin and Alan Jaeger

PHASE 1 >>
- **STRETCHING OUT** 10 to 14 days.
- Stretch out arm, progressively moving back.
- Eliminate stress on arm by keeping arc on throws.
- Listen to your arm! You can spend as few as 5 minutes or as many as 30 minutes throwing.
- You can throw every day in Phase 1 if you feel fine.
- Days 1 and 2, throw 60 to 90 feet for 5 to 10 minutes.

PHASE 2 >>
- **PULL DOWNS/STRENGTHENING** 10 to 14 days.
- Pull downs are throws on a line toward the end of a throwing program.
- Phase 2 should only be done after exceeding 90 to 100 percent of prior max distance.
- Execute 10 to 15 throws, starting from max distance and moving 10 feet after each throw.
- Listen to your arm! Pull downs can be done as few as 3 days a week or every day.
- End with relaxing in pocket/flat-ground screen work FB/CH.

PHASE 3 >>
- **GAME PREP** 10 to 14 days.
- Position players are now game ready.
- Continue strengthening through long toss and pull downs.
- If you are able to maintain your max distance for 10-15 throws, you are ready for bullpens.
- Begin splitting one bullpen FB/CH and one 10 to 15 pitch flat-ground session FB/CH per week.

- Listen to your arm! Take recommended light/off day after mound sessions.
- CB/SL can be thrown at the end of Phase 3.

HOW MUCH DO YOU REALLY KNOW ABOUT BASEBALL?

You probably know that in the United States, baseball is known as "the national pastime." But did you know …

- Baseball evolved from the British game of rounders and is a cousin to cricket.
- The first set of rules came from the New York Knickerbockers Base Ball Club.
- The first pro team was the Cincinnati Red Stockings.

This section provides a brief history of game's origins. It also provides an overview of the rules of the game. As someone who is serious about the game of baseball, you should read through this section carefully and learn more about the game you love to play.

HISTORY OF BASEBALL

Baseball is one of the most popular sports in North America. It is also popular in other parts of the world. Most competitive baseball is played in North America, the Caribbean, and the Far East.

Baseball evolved from the British game of rounders, which is a cousin to cricket. All three involve throwing a ball to some type of batter and the batter running around bases. Cricket is played on very short grass. During the American Civil War era (1850s and '60s), proper cricket fields were hard to find.

Because baseball could be played almost anywhere, more people played it. After the Civil War, baseball grew in popularity. General Abner Doubleday, a Union Civil War hero, used to be considered the inventor of baseball.

However, that story turned out to be false. Alexander Joy Cartwright is now commonly known as "the father of baseball." He wrote the first set of baseball rules in 1845 for a New York baseball club called the Knickerbockers. These rules were very close to the rules we play by today.

The first professional team was the Cincinnati Red Stockings, which formed in 1869. By the late 1800s, baseball had become known as the United States' "national pastime."

Two major leagues were formed: the National League in 1876 and the American League in 1903. The first modern World Series was played in 1903. It matched the Boston Americans of the American League against the Pittsburgh Pirates of the National League. Boston won.

At the beginning of the 20th century, baseball was a game dominated by great pitchers such as Walter Johnson, Christy Mathewson, and Cy Young. Large stadiums were built for many of the larger clubs, including Fenway Park in Boston and Wrigley Field and Comiskey Park in Chicago.

George "Babe" Ruth changed the game of baseball forever by introducing the power hitter. He hit 714 career home runs, almost 600 more than the previous career home run leader, Roger Connor. With such stars as Ruth, Ty Cobb, Lou Gehrig, and Joe DiMaggio, hitters took center stage.

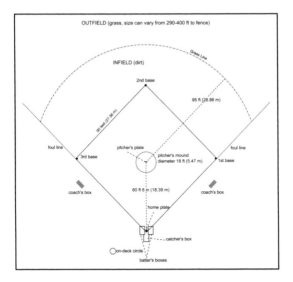

OUTFIELD (grass, size can vary from 290-400 ft to fence)

INFIELD (dirt)

Grass Line

2nd base

95 ft (28.88 m)

90 feet (27.36 m)

foul line

foul line

3rd base

pitcher's plate

pitcher's mound
diameter 18 ft (5.47 m)

1st base

coach's box

coach's box

60 ft 6 in (18.39 m)

home plate

catcher's box

on-deck circle

batter's boxes

In 1945, Brooklyn Dodgers general manager Branch Rickey signed Jackie Robinson to a contract for the 1946 season. It was the first time an African-American player was allowed to play in the major leagues.

After Robinson became a star player for the Dodgers, other African-American players were signed. Jackie Robinson later became a pivotal figure in the civil rights movement in the United States.

Baseball has not only maintained its position as the national pastime of the United States but also become an international game. It is played in more than 100 countries, including Canada, Cuba, Japan, Mexico, and China.

The Baseball "World Cup," the first international tournament, began in 1938 and continues to this day. Until 1996, only amateurs played in the World Cup. Now professionals may participate.

RULES OF BASEBALL

The *Official Baseball Rules* govern baseball games played by professional teams. The Official Playing Rules Committee is in charge of the rules, including making any changes to them.

Here's an overview of what you need to know in order to play baseball at a beginner's level. If you would like to read the latest version of the *Official Baseball Rules*, go to Major League Baseball's website at www.mlb.com.

THE BASEBALL FIELD

Baseball is played on a **baseball field**. A baseball field includes a **diamond**, which is the **infield**. It is bordered by foul lines. There are four **bases** in the infield: **first base, second base, third base**, and **home plate**.

Home plate is where the batter receives a pitch from the pitcher. It's also the final base that a player touches when he scores a run. The **batter's box** is where the batter stands during his time at bat.

The **outfield** is the grassed area beyond the infield grass line. It lies between the foul lines and is bordered by fences. A ball hit beyond the fences is a home run.

Foul territory is the entire area outside the foul lines.

The **pitcher's mound** is an elevated area in the middle of the infield. This is where the pitcher stands when he throws his pitches.

The **dugout** is the bench where the players sit, usually along the first- and third-base lines.

A **backstop** is the fence behind home plate, behind the catcher and umpire.

The size of the field depends on the level of play. In **Little League**, the distance between bases is 60 to 70 feet. In **Junior League, Senior League, Big League,** and **Major League** Baseball, the distance between bases is 90 feet.

POSITIONS

Infielder players comprise the first baseman, second baseman, third baseman, shortstop, pitcher, and catcher.

The **catcher** is the fielder who takes his position behind home plate and catches the pitch when the batter does not hit the ball.

The **pitcher** throws the ball to the batter, and the batter attempts to hit the ball and become a runner. A **pitch** is a ball delivered to the batter by the pitcher. The defensive players try to catch the ball after it is hit and put the batter and/or runners out.

An **outfielder** is a fielder who occupies a position in the outfield, which is the area of the playing field most distant from home plate.

Baseball is played between two teams of nine players each. The object of the game is to score more runs than the other team. Players score by working their way around the bases, from first base to second base to third base to home plate. A runner, or base runner, must touch each base when going around the infield. If he misses one, he has to go back to that base. The winner is the team with the most runs at the end of the game.

A baseball game starts when players of the home team take their positions on the field, the first batter of the visiting team takes his position in the batter's box, and the umpire calls, "Play!"

In baseball, the team that has the ball—and is pitching to the batter—is considered the **defense**. This is different from most other sports. The **batter** is an offensive player who takes his position in the batter's box and attempts to hit a ball thrown to him by the pitcher.

Each team bats and tries to score runs while the other team pitches and defends in the field. An **inning** is one portion of a game in which teams alternate on the field. Each team's time at bat is a half inning. The first half inning is called the "top" of the inning, during which the away team bats. The second half inning is called the "bottom" of the inning, when the home team bats.

Little League games have six innings. High school baseball games have seven. College and major league games have nine.

A batted baseball is **fair** if it lands in the field of play or if it touches or passes first or third base within fair territory. If the batter hits the ball successfully, he can do one of the following:

- Run to first base only. This is called a **single**.
- Run to first base, then second base. This is called a **double**.
- Continue past second base and run to third base. This is called a **triple**.
- Continue past third base to home plate. This is called a **home run**.

Any previous batters on one of the bases may advance to subsequent bases and finally home. A run is scored for each player of the batting team successfully reaching home plate.

A base runner can't pass a fellow runner in front of him when rounding the bases. He also can't run more than 3 feet away from his baseline to avoid being tagged out unless he is trying to avoid interference with a fielder.

If the batter does not hit the ball successfully, or if the ball is caught by the defending team before he reaches first base, he is **out**. When the batting team gets three **outs**, the other team bats.

OUTS

A batter is out when any of the following occur:

- He gets three **strikes**.
- He hits a ball that is caught before the ball hits the ground.

- The ball is thrown to the first baseman, and the first baseman touches the base with his foot while the ball is in his glove or hand.
- Any member of the fielding team tags the batter with the ball or the glove containing the ball before he safely reaches first base.
- Any member of the fielding team tags the batter with the ball or the glove containing the ball when the batter is on his way to second base, third base, or home.

STRIKES

A batter can get a strike in three different ways:

- He swings at a ball but doesn't hit it.
- He does NOT swing at a ball that is thrown into the **strike zone.** The strike zone is the space over home plate between the batter's shoulders and the top of his knees. In this case, the umpire will call it a strike.
- He swings at a ball and it becomes a **foul ball**.

A foul ball is one that rolls to the outside of the line from home plate to first base or outside the line from home plate to third base. A batter never receives a third and final strike for hitting a foul ball.

If foul balls are hit after two strikes are obtained, the batter keeps batting. The exception is a foul hit ball (or fair ball) caught before it strikes the ground. Then the batter is out.

BALLS AND WALKS

If the pitcher pitches to an area outside the strike zone, and the batter does not swing, the umpire will call "ball." If the umpire calls four balls before the batter strikes out, the batter will be given a "walk." In a walk, the batter is allowed to proceed to first base.

OVERRUNNING THE BASES

After a fair ball is hit, the batter tries to run to first base. If the batter is only going to run to first base, he is allowed to overrun the base and is considered "safe" if he touches the base before the first baseman catches the ball while standing on the base. The batter is still safe even if he is off base, as long as he runs straight past the base and turns to the right. If the batter touches first base and then heads to second base, he may be tagged out if he is not successful.

Tagging out occurs when a player from the fielding team touches the runner with the ball in hand or glove containing the ball. Also, players running from first to second or second to third base may always be tagged out if they overrun the base and the second or third baseman or other defender tags them.

FORCE-OUT VS. TAG-OUT SITUATIONS

Two runners from the batting team cannot occupy a base at the same time. Thus, if a runner is at first base and the next batter hits a fair ball, the runner on first must advance to at least second base.

This is known as a "force out at second" situation. In this case, the second baseman only has to tag the base before the runner arrives, rather than tag the runner.

If the second baseman has enough time, he can throw the ball to first base to get the hitter out as well. If this is successful, it is called a **double play**.

The **bases are loaded** when there are runners at each base. When this occurs, a force out is possible at first base, second base, third base, or home because all runners and batters are forced to advance to the next base.

A **ground ball** is a batted ball that rolls or bounces close to the ground.

A **pop fly ball** is a ball hit high into the air. Often, a fielder can catch it before it hits the ground. If a pop fly is caught before it hits the ground, the batter is automatically out.

Additionally, any runners starting to advance to another base before the ball is caught are out if the ball is thrown back to the baseman and he tags the base with his foot before the runner returns to the base.

STEALING BASES

An existing runner may run to the next base after the pitch is thrown and arrives at the catcher, even if the ball is not hit. This is known as a steal. In youth baseball leagues for ages 9 and younger, stealing bases is generally not allowed, although there are exceptions. For youth baseball leagues ages 9 to 12, stealing bases is allowed.

APPENDIX 2:
SPORTS NUTRITION GUIDELINES
FOR ATHLETES

*All of the **COMPLETE ATHLETE** sports nutrition guidelines were provided by Courtney M. Sullivan, founder of Nutrition for Body and Mind. Sullivan is a Registered Dietitian certified by the Academy of Nutrition and Dietetics and a Certified Personal Trainer certified by the National Academy of Sports Medicine. Below are more detailed guidelines as well as suggested meals and recipes developed by Sullivan.*

Nutrition is key to enhancing your athletic performance.

Young athletes with inadequate diets may have insufficient fuel for workouts, and/or nutrient deficiencies that can lead to fatigue, a compromised immune system, and possible injury. All of these will be reflected in their performance, regardless of their determination.

Proper intake of macronutrients and micronutrients is vital to enhance sports performance. Critical micronutrients include calcium, iron, folate, vitamin B6, and zinc.

CALCIUM

Poor calcium intake can lead to decreased bone mass and increased risk for stress fractures and possible bone-related injuries. The adequate intake of calcium for children who are 9 to 18 years old is 1,300 milligrams per day.

IRON

Important for its oxygen-carrying capacity, iron also plays a major role in energy metabolism of carbohydrates, protein, and fats. Young athletes with iron-deficiency anemia are at risk of performance inhibition as evidenced by fatigue, impaired immune function, and/or impaired cognitive reasoning. Foods rich in iron include red meat and enriched cereals and grains and should be coupled with fruits and vegetables that are high in vitamin C, which aids in iron absorption

FOLATE AND VITAMIN B6

Both are critical for amino acid metabolism. Good sources of each are enriched grain products and assorted animal products. Spinach, broccoli, lentils, and asparagus are also rich sources of folate. A vitamin B-complex deficiency can lead to fatigue, muscle soreness, and loss of cognitive function.

ZINC

Athletes are at risk of zinc deficiency due to poor consumption of foods rich in this mineral. Zinc plays a role in more than 300 enzymatic reactions in the body. It is also critical for wound healing, tissue growth and maintenance, and immune function. Dietary protein enhances zinc absorption and plays an important role in muscle recovery.

MACRONUTRIENTS

An increase in energy expenditure will require an increase in the intake of carbohydrates, protein and fats. However, you should consult with a registered dietitian to inquire about your customized macronutrient needs, which will be based on your height, weight, age, activity level, and gender.

Activity level is measured by the time (how long you exercise), type (your specific sport or training program), intensity (low, moderate, or high), and frequency (how often you perform this exercise/training). After determining these factors, your estimated calorie burn will be established.

Current research is showing that an increasing percentage of athletes are not consuming enough total calories, as well as total carbohydrate, in comparison to the amount of calories they are burning. Fluid intake is often inadequate as well, which alters the hydration status of young athletes. Therefore, it is very important to practice a pre- and post-workout nutrition regimen and rehydration program.

CARBOHYDRATES

For athletes, poor carbohydrate intake results in inadequate glycogen stores and fatigue, which compromises sports performance and forces your body to break down its own protein stores for fuel (through a process called gluconeogenesis). Carbohydrate is the preferred fuel source for athletic performance. Carbohydrate needs are based on body weight and intensity of activity.

- 3 to 5 grams of carbohydrate per kilogram body weight for very light intensity training
- 5 to 8 grams of carbohydrate per kilogram body weight for moderate or heavy training
- 8 to 9 grams of carbohydrate per kilogram body weight for pre-game loading (24 to 48 hours prior)
- 1.7 grams of carbohydrate per kilogram body weight for post-event refueling (within 2 to 3 hours)

PROTEIN

Protein is essential for athletes, with its role in muscle building and lean muscle maintenance, repair, and/or gain. It is important to note that an adequate protein intake and inadequate total calorie intake will inhibit protein balance and can still cause lean muscle breakdown. It is critical that athletes consume adequate total calories and protein to avoid this problem and maintain a healthy body weight. Vegetarians and vegans should be mindful of consuming adequate plant proteins. On the other end, consuming excess protein can lead to dehydration (it puts strain on the kidneys), weight gain (your body will store the excess protein that is not utilized as fat in the body), and calcium loss.

- Athletes who have just begun a training program need 1 to 1.5 grams of protein per kilogram of body weight
- Athletes participating in endurance sports require 1.2 to 1.4 grams of protein per kilogram of body weight

FAT

Fat is essential for light- to moderate-intensity exercise and for absorption of fat-soluble vitamins.

Low-fat diets are not encouraged. Adequate heart-healthy fats such as monounsaturated and polyunsaturated fats should make up 20 to 30 percent of your total calories.

Lowering the amount of saturated fat and trans fat (the unhealthy fats) is highly encouraged. Ideally, your diet should consist of less than 7percent of total calories from saturated fat and, preferably, no trans fat.

Maintaining proper fluid balance is critical to athletic performance and avoiding early fatigue and heat exhaustion. Signs of dehydration include dark urine, small urine output, muscle cramps, increased heart rate, headaches, nausea, and vomiting.

- Be sure to consume 16 to 24 ounces of fluid for every pound lost via sweat during exercise.
- For activities that are less than 60 minutes, hydrate with water.
- For activities that are greater than 60 minutes, hydrate with a sports beverage containing 6 to 8 percent carbohydrate to replete electrolytes and energy.

GENERAL GUIDELINES

- All athletes should consume five or more balanced meals spread throughout the day, every 3 to 4 hours.
- Eating every 3 hours helps to maintain your metabolic rate, lower-body fat, lower serum lipid levels (cholesterol), decrease stress hormone production, lower insulin response, and improve glucose tolerance (especially if you are prediabetic, diabetic currently, or have diabetes in your family history).
- Meals should be eaten 2 to 3 hours before practice or games, and snacks eaten 1 to 1.5 hours before practice or games.
- Eat when you're hungry to prevent lean muscle breakdown and stop when you're full to prevent being sluggish. Listen to your intuitive eating cues, which help to do the following:

- — Maintain blood sugar and insulin control
- — Regulate appetite
- — Improve concentration
- — Gain lean-muscle mass
- — Enhance muscle in the recovery process
  (i.e., repairing and rebuilding of muscles)

- Eat breakfast within 30 minutes of waking to prevent lean muscle breakdown, increase energy and concentration, and maintain good blood sugar control.
- Choose whole grains, fresh fruit, and lean protein.
- Eat well-balanced meals and snacks consisting of carbohydrates, lean proteins, and heart healthy fats.
- Drink a protein shake or eat a snack or meal that has equal amounts of protein and carbohydrates within 30 minutes of a workout.
- Choose fresh, whole foods when possible instead of processed foods that are packaged or refined to increase nutritional value. Especially avoid foods that are high in sugar or trans fats.

MEAL PLANNING

BREAKFAST >> This is the most important meal of the day so don't skip it! You are coming from an overnight fast and will wake up with low blood sugar (by default). Breakfast literally means to "break the fast." You need to focus on eating breakfast within 30 minutes of waking to prevent lean muscle breakdown, increase energy and concentration, and maintain good blood sugar control.

Start your morning with 8 to 12 ounces of water with a squeeze of lemon to rehydrate and reduce stomach acidity. Choose whole grains, fresh fruit, and lean protein. Although many breakfast choices are focused around carbohydrates, it is important to include a good source of protein for satiety and lean muscle gain or maintenance.

EXAMPLE BREAKFAST MEAL >> Try 1 to 2 scrambled eggs (cage-free preferred), 1 slice of whole-grain toast with $1/4$ avocado (spread on top of toast). Add a side of sliced tomatoes and $1/2$ cup low-fat cottage cheese (for added protein as needed). If you're trying to gain weight, adding a protein shake is also ideal.

SNACK >> Choose a snack consisting of lean protein, fresh fruit, and a whole-grain carbohydrate. You can add essential, heart-healthy fat as needed.

EXAMPLE MID-MORNING SNACK/MEAL >> Select a medium-size organic apple (i.e., the size of a tennis ball) with 2 tablespoons of natural almond butter or peanut butter and 1 cup nonfat or low-fat plain Greek yogurt. Optional: add sprinkled cinnamon and $1/2$ cup blueberries to yogurt.

LUNCH >> Eat a well-balanced meal consisting of carbohydrates (whole grains, not refined white flours or sugars) and lean proteins with a side of fresh or steamed vegetables and heart-healthy fats (omega-3s).

EXAMPLE LUNCH MEAL >> Try 3-4 ounces of boneless, skinless chicken breast, $1/2$ to 1 cup cooked brown rice, and a side (roughly 1 cup) of steamed mixed vegetables or green vegetable of choice (e.g., broccoli, asparagus, Brussel sprouts, zucchini, etc.). Add a piece of fresh fruit such as a medium-size orange (size of tennis ball).

SNACK >> Choose a snack consisting of a lean protein, fresh vegetable, and whole-grain carbohydrate.

Avoid consuming foods high in fat or excessive amounts of fiber or protein before a practice or game because these foods digest slowly. Your body needs foods that are higher in carbohydrates, which yield readily available energy for working muscles and also contain high nutrient/water density to increase hydration.

EXAMPLE AFTERNOON SNACK/MEAL >> Eat 1 slice of whole-grain toast with hummus (1 to 2 tablespoons) and 2 thin slices of turkey with sliced cucumber and tomato. You can eat this open-faced or add another piece of whole-grain toast for additional carbohydrates. This depends on your current age, macronutrient needs, and training regimen.

DINNER >> Eat a well-balanced meal consisting of carbohydrates (whole grains, not refined white flours or sugars) and lean proteins, adding fresh or steamed vegetables and heart-healthy fats (omega-3s).

EXAMPLE DINNER MEAL >> Select 3 to 4 ounces of lean protein (e.g., fish, chicken, turkey, etc.), $1/2$ to 1 cup cooked quinoa or baked/sweet potato with skin, and a side salad (e.g., kale/spinach/or mixed greens with chopped tomato, garbanzo or kidney beans, shredded carrots, chopped broccoli, avocado, feta cheese, and a light balsamic vinaigrette).

POST WORKOUT (WITHIN 30 MINUTES) >> Consume a protein shake or balanced intake of protein and carbohydrates to repair your muscles overnight and restore glycogen that was used during your practice or game so that you are prepared to get after it tomorrow! (See protein shake recipes that follow for recovery nutrition.)

NIGHTTIME (BEFORE BED) SNACK » The myths that you should not eat after 7 PM or 2 hours before bed do not apply to you! You are an athlete; therefore, you need to fuel your body properly to optimize your athletic performance.

EXAMPLE NIGHTTIME SNACK MEAL » Try 1 to 2 tablespoons of almond butter or natural peanut butter with $1/2$ cup organic raspberries or strawberries. *Optional:* Add 1 cup nonfat plain Greek yogurt.

HYDRATION

- 14 to 22 ounces (2+ cups) 2 hours before exercise
- 8 ounces 10 to 20 minutes before exercise
- 6 to 8 ounces every 15 to 20 minutes during practice
- 16 to 24 ounces (2 to 3 cups) for every 1 pound lost within 2 hours of practice.
- Sodium (Na) -0.5 to -0.7 g/L in exercise lastinggreater than 1 hour (500 mg Na/hour for distance runners/ heavy sweaters)Increased risk of hyponatremia (low sodium can have dangerous effects on the body)

*Consume 24 ounces of fluid for every pound lost via sweat. Pay attention to internal cues (e.g., headaches) or external cues (e.g., urine color) to monitor hydration status. If you have a headache, you are most likely already gretater than 10percent dehydrated.

Your urine should be light yellow color or clear. If it is dark yellow or black, you are dehydrated and need to increase your fluids (and overall electrolytes, including sodium, potassium, calcium, and magnesium) drastically.

---

*Adapted from guidelines provided by the American College of Sports Medicine (ACSM)

PHYSICAL/MENTAL EFFECTS OF DEHYDRATION >>

- Decreased muscle strength, speed, stamina, energy, cognitive processes
- Increased risk of injury

BENEFITS OF ADEQUATE FLUIDS >>

- Decreased heart rate, perceived exertion
- Increased stroke volume, cardiac output, skin blood flow, and improved athletic performance

ADDITIONAL TIPS AND TRICKS

AVOID "BOTTOM-HEAVY DIETS." This is defined as eating $2/3$ of your total daily caloric intake in the afternoon or evening (anytime between 3 to 10 PM). The timing in which you consume your meals will affect your body composition.

Studies show that an athlete who consumes a "bottom-heavy diet" will have a higher body fat percentage than another athlete who consumes his or her meals throughout the day every 3 to 4 hours (even if both athletes are consuming the same total calories and following the same training regimen). You need to eat to fuel your body for when it needs energy for optimal metabolism, lean muscle gain, and optimal performance. You may be skilled in soccer, but mastering your nutrition will help take you to the next level.

JOIN THE CONVERSATION!

Share your favorite game-day recipes in the **COMPLETE ATHLETE** app!

LEVELS 1-5

MACRONUTRIENTS	HEALTHY FOODS FOR LEAN-MUSCLE GAIN
CARBOHYDRATES	Fresh and dried fruits, fresh vegetables (peas, corn, potatoes topped with extra virgin olive oil), whole-grain breads, cornbread, multigrain muffins, bagels, brown/wild/jasmine rice, pasta/gluten-free pasta, cereal, steel-cut oatmeal, granola
PROTEINS	Eggs, chicken, turkey, fish, tuna, salmon, lean beef, pork tenderloin, Greek yogurt, milk (or nondairy high protein substitutes), beans, soybeans, nuts, nut butters, seeds, seed butters
FATS	Nuts and seeds (flaxseeds, chia seeds, hemp seeds, pumpkin seeds, etc.) olives, hummus, avocados, guacamole, oils (olive, canola, flaxseed, grapeseed, coconut, etc.) cheese

TIMING OF MEALS (FOR LEVELS 1-5) >> Eating smaller and more frequent meals is ideal for proper digestion, metabolism, and lean-muscle weight gain. Eating frequently yields high energy and stable blood sugar levels. Waiting too long between meals can lead to lean-muscle breakdown and weight loss. Athletes with poor nutrition are more prone to injury, especially during periods of growth and development or when their bones are strengthening or becoming more dense.

NUTRITION REGIMEN: NIGHT BEFORE GAME DAY

Avoid greasy or fried foods that are high in fat. Avoid high amounts of sugar, or refined carbohydrates, which can also make you feel sluggish. "Carb loading" is not necessary. Instead, eat a balanced meal containing lean protein, whole grain carbohydrates, and steamed vegetables. Add a protein shake for dessert (if needed).

MACRONUTRIENT SUGGESTIONS

CARBOHYDRATES >> Higher fiber foods (i.e., lower Glycemic Index), such as whole-grain bread, brown rice, whole-grain pasta, (or gluten-free versions), beans, starchy vegetables (e.g., corn, peas, potatoes), quinoa, and cereal.

PROTEINS >> Chicken, turkey, or fish (e.g., wild salmon, tuna, trout, mackerel, or sardines, which are high in heart healthy omega-3 fatty acids.)

FATS >> Low-fat cheese, nuts/nut butters (e.g., natural peanut butter or almond butter), avocado, seeds, oils (e.g., extra-virgin olive oil, canola oil, grapeseed oil, flaxseed oil.)

VEGETABLES >> All green vegetables are preferable.

AVOID PACKAGED, PROCESSED, AND REFINED FOODS THAT ARE HIGH IN SUGAR OR TRANS FAT >> These foods are high in preservatives and artificial ingredients that our bodies do not process well and may cause an upset stomach. These foods may provide convenience and quick energy, but they will ultimately lead to a "crash" or feeling of fatigue about 1 hour after consumption due to the quick rise and fall of your blood sugar levels.

Artificial trans-fatty acids are unhealthy fats that are added to foods to increase their shelf life (how long they are "safe" to eat). Be sure to look at the ingredient list below the nutrition facts label for "partially or fully hydrogenated oils," which means there is trans fat in the product and you should avoid it. Trans fat raises your LDL (bad cholesterol) and lowers your HDL (good cholesterol), which can increase your risk of heart disease, stroke, or Type-II Diabetes.

IDEAL DINNER MEAL BEFORE GAME DAY NO. 1

PROTEIN >> Boneless, skinless chicken breast (portion: 3 to 6 ounces, depending on the athlete level.)

CARBOHYDRATE >> Brown rice (portion: $1/2$ to $1^1/2$ cups cooked, depending on the athlete level.)

VEGETABLE >> Side salad with organic spinach leaves, chopped cucumbers, carrots, tomato, and a light olive oil and vinegar dressing.

IDEAL DINNER MEAL BEFORE GAME DAY NO. 2

PROTEIN >> Ground turkey (portion: 3 to 6 ounces, depending on the athlete level)

CARBOHYDRATE >> Baked potato (1 medium-size) with a dollop of low-fat Greek yogurt instead of sour cream (optional) or brown rice and quinoa pasta (portion: $^1/_2$ to $1^1/_2$ cups cooked depending on the athlete level)

VEGETABLE >> Steamed broccoli and mushrooms (portion: 1 to 2 cups, depending on the athlete level)

NUTRITION REGIMEN: MORNING OF GAME

Avoid high-fat or high-protein foods the morning of game day, which are more difficult for the body to digest. Carbohydrates provide the best source of readily available energy for the body. Dairy products can be tolerated in a small amount but can cause gastrointestinal discomfort (upset stomach) when consumed in a larger amount. The body will use carbohydrates as its first source of energy.

MACRONUTRIENT SUGGESTIONS

CARBOHYDRATES >> Lower-fiber foods (higher glycemic index), cream of rice, oatmeal with 2 grams of fiber or less, rice cereal (dry), bread (with 2 grams of fiber), or plain bagel

PROTEINS >> Eggs/egg whites, protein shakes (made with whey protein, pea protein, vegan protein, hemp protein, etc.), low-fat plain Greek yogurt.

FATS >> Nuts/nut butters (e.g., peanut butter, almond butter, cashew butter, sunflower-seed butter), seeds, avocado.

FRUITS >> 1 medium-size piece of fresh fruit (e.g., banana, apple, kiwi, peach, pear, nectarine, plum)

Peanut butter (or almond butter) and jelly (or honey) sandwich on whole-wheat bread with a sliced banana

1 cup low-fat plain Greek yogurt** with $1/2$ cup organic blueberries or a banana with 1 cup Rice Chex cereal. Avoid high-fiber cereals, such as Kashi, which will cause an upset stomach.

NOTE >> Greek yogurt contains 20 grams of protein per cup and healthy probiotics, which increase immunity and aid in proper digestion. It is important to get the low-fat or nonfat version (to avoid the high saturated fat content) and plain (to avoid the 20 to 22 grams of added sugar in the flavored varieties.)

CAFFEINE >> Caffeine has been proven to be one of the best ergogenic aids and is known to help athletes train harder and longer. Caffeine stimulates the brain and contributes to clearer thinking and greater concentration. If you like coffee or tea, consume caffeine at least 1 hour before practice or a game.

Recommendation: 1 to 3 milligrams per kilogram of body weight (e.g., 200 milligrams for a 150-pound man). Do not consume caffeine in the form of energy drinks or soda because they have concentrated sources of sugar, which cancel out the health benefits. Coffee and green tea are natural sources of caffeine and provide a high anti-oxidant value (cancer fighting). Make sure to only add a dash of honey, agave, or milk (no added sugar).

---

*Drink fluids with carbohydrate and electrolytes if exercise exceeds 1 hour for improved performance and decreased fatigue.

- 14 to 22 ounces (2+ cups) 2 hours before exercise
- 8 ounces 10 to 20 minutes before exercise
- 6 to 8 ounces every 15 to 20 minutes during practice
- 16 to 24 ounces (2 to 3 cups) for every 1 pound lost within 2 hours of practice
- Sodium (Na) -0.5 to -0.7 g/L in exercise lasting greater than 1 hour (500 mg Na/hour for distance runners/heavy sweaters)—Increased risk of hyponatremia (low sodium can have dangerous effects on the body)

* Consume 24 ounces of fluid for every 1 pound lost via sweat. Pay attention to internal cues (i.e., headaches) or external cues (i.e., urine color) to monitor hydration status. If you have a headache, you are most likely already greater than 10 percent dehydrated.

Your urine should be light yellow color or clear. If it is dark yellow or black, you are dehydrated and need to increase your fluids (and overall electrolytes, including sodium, potassium, calcium, and magnesium) drastically.

PHYSICAL / MENTAL EFFECTS OF DEHYDRATION

- Decreased muscle strength, speed, stamina, energy, cognitive processes
- Increased risk of injury

BENEFITS OF ADEQUATE FLUIDS

- Decreased heart rate, perceived exertion
- Increased stroke volume, cardiac output, skin blood flow, and improved athletic performance

TRADER JOE'S TREK MIX »

- Trader Joe's Trek Mix—sold in individual packs.
- Trader Joe's raw mixed nuts or make your own nut trail mix. Choose from almonds, pistachios, pecans, walnuts, hazelnuts, Brazil nuts, cashews. Add dried fruit: cranberries, raisins, apricots, blueberries, goji berries, acai berries, or mango pieces.

- 100 percent whole-wheat or Ezekiel 4:9 bread with all-natural peanut butter or almond butter (optional: add a sliced banana and raspberry jam).

- Granola bars: Choose one that is higher in protein and carbohydrates and low-fat because fat digests slowly and will not provide the quick energy you need for practice/your game. Good choices include Think Thin protein bars (gluten free, sugar free), Pure Protein bars, Strong and KIND bars, Greens+ protein and energy bars, Kashi granola bars (many flavors).
- Cereal (containing >3 g fiber per serving) can be eaten dry or with $1/2$ cup almond milk (examples: Kashi Go Lean, Kashi Crunch, Kashi Heart to Heart, Optimum Wheat, Optimum Slim, shredded wheat, Nature's Best and Nature's Path cereals, Barbara's Shredded Spoonfuls, Barbara's Puffins, and Kellogg's Special K or Rice Chex/puffs if you're looking for a lower-fiber cereal)
- Healthier chips / crackers: reduced guilt pita chips, Lundberg brown rice chips, Trader Joe's spicy soy flaxseed chips, vegetable chips, raisin rosemary crisps, popcorn chips, edamame crackers, bite-size pita crackers, Blue Diamond nut thins, Kashi 7 grain

crackers, high-fiber Wasa crackers, Mary's Gone gluten-free or whole-wheat crackers (Mix any of these with hummus, yogurt chive dip, spinach dip, fresh salsa or homemade guacamole.)

- Drinkable yogurt or Chobani, Fage, or Trader Joe's single-serving Greek yogurts (if eaten within 2 hours) Graham crackers with almond butter or peanut butter spread on top.
- String cheese (if eaten within 2 hours)
- Beef jerky or low-sodium turkey jerky with no nitrates or preservatives added.
- Fresh, portable fruit (i.e., apple, banana, pear, peach, nectarine, apricot, orange, blood orange, tangerine, plum, grapes, kiwi, berries, etc.)
- English muffin/wheat wrap with almond butter or natural peanut butte.
- Multigrain, sesame seed, or 100 percent whole-wheat bagel with part- skim mozzarella cheese or reduced-fat vegetable cream cheese (can replace with hummus or Greek yogurt if eaten within 1 to 2 hours of preparation)
- Cooked quinoa (place in large container and snack on the plane with veggies)
- Yogurt-covered raisins or pretzels.
- Hard-boiled eggs (if eaten within 2 hours)
- Build your own sandwich: Whole-grain dinner roll or 2 slices whole-wheat bread with lean protein (sliced turkey, chicken, or ham), 1 slice low-fat provolone cheese, mustard or hummus, lettuce, tomato, and avocado (optional)
- Almond butter and jelly/raspberry preserve sandwich on wheat bread or Ezekiel 4:9 bread for breakfast/snack on the go.
- Whole-wheat pretzels (dip in all-natural peanut butter for sweet and salty taste) or peanut butter-filled pretzels
- Meal-replacement shakes (made with water or coconut

water and whey protein, RAW protein, OR Trader Joe's pure protein shakes, which have 21 grams of protein and come in chocolate or vanilla flavors).

NOTE >> Shakes only require a mixer/shaker to blend the protein and beverage. Use 1 percent Chocolate milk.

MILK PROTEINS >> Whey and casein stimulate muscle-protein synthesis and prevent muscle breakdown.

HIGH-PROTEIN SHAKE RECIPES

Add natural whey protein or plant-based protein (pea protein or vegan Vega) powder to any of the following smoothies that don't already include protein powder. You can alternate between the following milks and milk substitutes: nonfat organic milk, 2 percent organic milk, or unsweetened versions of almond, coconut, hemp, or rice milk.

To increase calories, use a larger serving of the nuts or nut butters and seeds or seed butters. To reduce carbohydrates, use a smaller serving of fresh or dried fruit (bananas, dates, etc.). To increase fiber and nutrients without adding calories, add more leafy greens such as kale or spinach.

8 ounces unsweetened coconut milk
$^1/_2$ banana
2 tablespoons hemp seeds
1 to 2 tablespoons chia seeds
2 dates
Sprinkle of nutmeg

NUTRITION FACTS >> 400 calories, 16 grams fat (mono-
and polyunsaturated fat), 25 grams carbohydrate, 13 grams
fiber, 18 grams protein (add 10 grams protein powder as
needed to make it 28 grams protein total)

PROTEIN POWER UP

8 ounces Silk unsweetened almond milk
1 scoop whey or pea protein powder
$^1/_2$ cup nonfat plain Greek yogurt
2 tablespoon almond butter
$^1/_2$ banana
Sprinkle of cinnamon

NUTRITION FACTS >> 350 calories, 20 grams fat (mono-
and polyunsaturated fat), 14 grams carbohydrate, 5 grams
fiber, 43 grams protein

BERRY BLAST

8 ounces Silk unsweetened almond milk
$1/2$ cup blueberries
$1/2$ cup raspberries
$1/2$ cup blackberries
1 ounce raw, unsalted walnuts
1 tablespoon ground flaxseeds (Bob's Red Mill brand)

NUTRITION FACTS » 400 calories, 18 grams fat (mono- and polyunsaturated fat), 30 grams carbohydrate, 18 grams fiber, 10 grams protein (add 10 to 20 grams protein powder as needed to make it 20 to 30 grams protein total).

IMMUNE BOOSTER

8 ounces unsweetened coconut milk
1 scoop pea protein powder
1 cup chopped kale
$1/2$ cup frozen mango chunks
2 dates
Slivers of fresh ginger
Sprinkle of coconut flakes

NUTRITION FACTS » 360 calories, 8.5 grams fat (mono- and polyunsaturated fat), 35 grams carbohydrate, 10 grams fiber, 37 grams protein

8 ounces coconut water
1 to 2 teaspoons maca powder
1 teasponn turmeric powder
$^1/_2$ avocado
$^1/_2$ cup frozen pineapple chunks
$^1/_2$ cup frozen organic blueberries
1 cup spinach leaves
Touch of mint

NUTRITION FACTS >> 260 calories, 13 grams fat (mono-unsaturated fat), 31 grams carbohydrate, 14 grams fiber, 8 grams protein (add scoop of protein powder, 20 grams, to make 28 grams protein total).

DETOX

8 ounces coconut water
1 banana
$^1/_2$ pear
$^1/_2$ cup chopped cucumber
1 cup chopped kale
1 fresh squeezed lemon
Touch of cilantro
Sprinkle of cayenne pepper (optional for spice/heat)

NUTRITION FACTS >> 240 calories, 0 grams fat, 37 grams carbohydrate, 8 grams fiber, 7.5 grams protein (add scoop of protein powder, 20 grams, to make 28 grams protein total).

ANTIOXIDANT

8 ounces unsweetened coconut milk
$1/2$ cup strawberries
$1/2$ cup blueberries
1 banana
$1/2$ cup shredded carrot
1 cup spinach leaves
1 tablespoon goji berries

NUTRITION FACTS » 340 calories, 4.5 grams fat (monounsaturated fat), 45 grams carbohydrate, 25 grams fiber, 9 grams protein (add scoop of protein powder, 20 grams, to make 29 grams protein total)

BLISS

8 ounces Silk unsweetened vanilla almond milk
1 scoop vanilla whey protein powder
1 tablespoon cacao powder
$1/2$ banana
2 dates
1 ounce cashews
Sprinkle of cinnamon & nutmeg

NUTRITION FACTS » 375 calories, 20 grams fat (monounsaturated fat), 30 grams carbohydrate, 12 grams fiber, 35 grams protein.

MEET THE TEAM

TREVOR HOFFMAN is an 18-year Major League pitcher, including 16 years with the San Diego Padres, as well as time with the Florida Marlins and Milwaukee Brewers. He has the second-most career saves in MLB history (601 in 677 opportunities).

He is a seven-time All-Star who finished in the top 10 in Cy Young voting and in the top 25 MVP voting on four separate occasions each. The "Trevor Hoffman National League Reliever of the Year Award" is named in his honor. Following his retirement in January 2011, Hoffman has served as special assistant to the president and CEO of the Padres, upper-level pitching coordinator, and is currently a senior advisor to baseball operations.

His jersey was only the fifth Padres jersey ever to be retired. Hoffman has been deeply involved with various community organizations since joining the Padres in 1993. He has worked with the National Kidney Foundation, Rady Children's Hospital, and a number of community and military outreach programs in his native southern California. He and his wife have three sons: Brody, Quinn, and Wyatt.

DAVE COGGIN from Upland, California, was a two-sport All-American in high school in both football and baseball. He was recruited heavily by D-1 schools on both coasts but signed with the Philadelphia Phillies right out of high school after being drafted in the first round.

Coggin played 12 years of professional baseball before launching Performance Fitness for Athletes (PFA), one of the premiere baseball training facilities in the nation.

PFA accommodates both professionals and amateurs and boasts more than 100 high school players who have gone on to play college baseball in all divisions and more than 60 players who have been drafted into the pros from both high school and college.

DON YAEGER is a nationally acclaimed motivational speaker, longtime associate editor of *Sports Illustrated*, and author of 25 books, 10 of which have become *New York Times* best sellers. Don has written books with Hall of Fame running back Walter Payton, UCLA basketball coach John Wooden, baseball legends John Smoltz and Tug McGraw, and football stars Warrick Dunn and Michael Oher (featured in the movie *The Blind Side*), among others.

He teamed with Fox News anchor Brian Kilmeade to pen the 2013 best seller *George Washington's Secret Six*, a look at the citizen spy ring that helped win the Revolutionary War, and then again in 2015 for *Thomas Jefferson and the Tripoli Pirates: The Forgotten War that Changed American History*.

Don left *Sports Illustrated* in 2008 to pursue a motivational speaking career that has allowed him to share stories learned from the greatest winners of our generation. In this capacity, he is able to share lessons from nearly three decades of studying how highly successful athletes and business professionals think, prepare, work, and live in order to consistently achieve greatness both on and off the field.

MIKE MARTIN has been head baseball coach of the Florida State Seminoles since 1980 and is currently the second-winningest coach in all of Division I baseball.

With 15 College World Series appearances, 24 50-win seasons, and 13 Conference *Coach of the Year* awards, Martin has led the Seminoles on their climb to become a college baseball powerhouse. Under Martin's leadership, Florida State has won the ACC Sportsmanship Award multiple times and is consistently ranked at or near the top of conference rankings for GPA, with more than 60 FSU baseball players having been selected to the Academic Team of Distinction since 2006.

Martin has coached nearly 200 players who have gone on to the Major League Draft, with more than 20 going in the first round. He has coached eight National Players of the Year and four Golden Spikes Award winners, as well as being named to the Florida Sports Hall of Fame in 2005 and the American Baseball Coaches Association Hall of Fame in 2007. He is a proud father and grandfather.

JON OLSEN is a right handed pitcher playing for the UCLA Bruins. Originally from Rancho Cucamonga, California, he decided to attend UCLA after a decorated high school career because he felt there was no better option for academics and athletics.

DANIEL ROBERTSON is a shortstop with the Tampa Bay Rays organization. After playing for Upland High School in Upland, California, Robertson was taken in the first round of the 2012 Major League Baseball Draft by the Oakland Athletics.

BRENTON SULLIVAN is CEO and cofounder of FieldLevel, which connects high school athletes to college and university programs. He oversees FieldLevel's overall strategic vision and product roadmap. He works closely with the engineering team to lead product innovation.

Named to the *Los Angeles Business Journal's* "Twenty in Their 20s," Sullivan previously worked at University of Southern California as director of operations for the varsity baseball team. Prior to working at USC, Sullivan was a production assistant at Fox Sports, building highlights for both "The Final Score" and "Fox NFL Sunday".

ACKNOWLEDGMENTS

I would like first to thank Gary Jabara for his vision and dedication to making this book possible. Without him pushing and encouraging me to work on this, it would have just been another good idea that never was put on paper. He has been the real force behind everything with this project.

I also want to thank the many athletes that have contributed time and stories to this book. Most special to this project was Trevor Hoffman; thank you for opening your heart and sharing with so many what it took and who helped you reach the very top of the baseball community.

You are truly a Level 5 athlete and a Hall of Famer both on and off the field. Thank you, as well, to Daniel Robertson for sharing his stories and taking time to be photographed while playing in a game in Texas versus the Rangers. You are all inspiring to a whole new generation of ballplayers.

Thank you to the team behind the scenes as well. Ziad and Walid Khoury have been like brothers to me, and it seems at times that I have seen them more than my family while working on this series. Thank you, as well, to my team at Performance Fitness for Athletes for picking up my slack when I was working on **COMPLETE ATHLETE**, especially my assistant Bobby O'Neill.

And, finally, to all the parents, coaches, and athletes with whom I have had the enjoyment of working with my whole life—my deepest appreciation.

Without you, I would have no stories to share.

You have always given me the energy, passion, and enthusiasm to answer your call.

I am so blessed to be able to share our experiences in this book. It is such an uncertain time for baseball players and injuries are an epidemic; without the knowledge of this book I fear the cycle will continue to negatively affect the growth of this amazing sport.

We need to build up our athletes so they can play longer, utilize their experiences, stories, relationships, and friendships long after their on-field career is over, and pass along what it takes to become a **COMPLETE ATHLETE**.